Heinrich St. A. von Liaño

The Church of God and the Bishops

Heinrich St. A. von Liaño

The Church of God and the Bishops

ISBN/EAN: 9783743324831

Manufactured in Europe, USA, Canada, Australia, Japa

Cover: Foto ©ninafisch / pixelio.de

Manufactured and distributed by brebook publishing software (www.brebook.com)

Heinrich St. A. von Liaño

The Church of God and the Bishops

THE CHURCH OF GOD AND THE BISHOPS

AN ESSAY SUGGESTED BY THE CONVOCATION OF THE VATICAN COUNCIL

BY

HENRY ST. A. VON LIAÑO

AUTHORISED TRANSLATION

RIVINGTONS
London, Oxford, and Cambridge
POTT AND AMERY, NEW YORK
1870

CONTENTS

	PAGE
NOTICE TO THE ENGLISH TRANSLATION . . .	vii
PREFACE	1
INTRODUCTION, ON THE RELIGIOUS QUESTION OF OUR DAY	5
SECTION I	17
SECTION II	34
APPENDIX I	87
APPENDIX II	95
SUPPLEMENT TO THE SECOND EDITION . . .	145

NOTICE

TO THE ENGLISH TRANSLATION

THE Author of this little work is a Spanish Catholic of noble family, now resident at Munich, where he is well known for his devout and ascetic life, his deep religious convictions, and his zealous attachment to his Church, which he believes—as will be seen from the following pages — to be just now passing through a peculiarly trying and perilous crisis.

The present translation was undertaken with the sanction and kind encouragement of the Author. It is published in the belief that there are many English readers, both Protestant and

Catholic, who will be glad of the opportunity of studying Señor von Liaño's weighty words in their own language. Should this anticipation be realised, a translation of a later essay of his, on the distinction between dogma and opinion, (*Dogma und Schulmeinung*)—written with particular reference to the proposed erection of Papal Infallibility and the Assumption of the Blessed Virgin into articles of faith—may perhaps be offered to the public hereafter.

PREFACE

THE Author of this little work, in this hour of peril, and in presence of a party which has been permitted in our days, in a manner hitherto unheard of, to disseminate its own ideas as the expression of Church truth, is convinced that he represents the most sacred interests of his Church, to which he is in all things and most unreservedly devoted.

He has written because he knows what immeasurable dangers threaten us, should the plans of that school be realised, even in part.

He knows that he can only very imperfectly fulfil the task which he has undertaken from a sense of duty, and he laments that, in consequence of the exceedingly deplorable circumstances of the times, no better champions of these views have as yet stepped forward.

He entreats the chief pastors of the Church, and the pastors of the second order, to weigh what he lays before them by the light of the genuine tradition of the Church, and in the balance of the sanctuary.

He addresses the same request to the great upholders and representatives of true learning, be they priests or members of the Catholic laity. May they ever bear in mind that one of the most impressive, most real, and most important effects of the spirit of Christianity is to be recognised in the immense elevation of the sciences, as well as of art, during the Christian era, notwithstanding the natural greatness of the intellectual heroes of ante-Christian antiquity—and may they ever bear in mind the obligations thus laid upon them.

This work is, however, primarily addressed to believing Church-loving Catholics, who do not belong to the ranks of the clergy, or of the learned among the laity, but who are men of business, and who are, or expect to be, fathers of families, and likewise to those Christian and Catholic maidens and wives who know and love their religion, who are now called upon, in the spheres of activity belonging to their sex, to help, in the most various ways, to feed and tend the sacred fire. The author trusts that if his voice is not perhaps the fittest to address these last, yet, in default of a more able defender of the pure and simple truth, he may serve them as a guide on the vital question at issue. He begs both men and women to read his little work with prayer to the Spirit of Truth, of Righteousness and of Love,—the Holy Ghost,—and to weigh well what it contains, without allowing themselves to be influenced by prejudices, imbibed perhaps in early years, but which can no longer be cherished without exposing the soul without defence to the greatest dangers.

The author also begs all well-intentioned Protestants, that is, those who wish to hold fast positive Christianity, to pay attention to his little work. He does not believe that they have reason to expect their opinions to be represented at Worms;* and it may therefore appear to them that they are the more called upon to consider the arguments laid before them in these pages, which the reader will find are not of the author's invention. Were this the case, in this most sacred matter, they would only deserve contempt.

Finally, the author begs all religious statesmen, to whatever confession they may belong, who are only willing to ponder the seriousness of the situation, and are equitable enough to be able to place themselves at the point of view of a Catholic, who is one, not merely according to the statistics of the census table, and who knows both the true nature and the genuine doctrine of his Church, to read his little work, especially the note on "Curialism," and the second appendix, to inquire into the truth of its contents, and to weigh them well.

May the blessing of God rest on this honest endeavour!

* This has since proved only too true.

INTRODUCTION

ON THE RELIGIOUS QUESTION OF OUR DAY

OUR age is characterised by an universal absence of fixed principles in all departments of morals.

Men scarcely know any longer what constitutes their earthly country; what is suitable to its nature and peculiarities; what is required by right and justice, and what alone can advance and secure the true interests of this earthly country; what patriotic duty requires of them.

Still less do they know what is required of them by the highest, by the only true and universal law —by religion.

Believers in Christianity and true sons of the

Catholic Church, we can only have Christianity and the Catholic faith in view, while we seek for landmarks to guide us, especially on the eve of an event which must be looked upon as likely to have important consequences, and with regard to which no true son of our Holy Mother the Church can remain indifferent, or even passive, if he is duly instructed in the nature and life of the Church, and as to her relations with society at large.

"*Jampridem equidem vera rerum vocabula amisimus.*" Truly we have long since unlearned the habit of giving things their right names. These words, which, if we mistake not, Sallust places in the mouth of the elder Cato to describe, in the shortest and most emphatic manner, the decline of morals in ancient Rome, are terribly true in our days.

Only now and then is anything called by its right name; and this almost universal incapacity to name rightly things, persons, and institutions, which has its origin in indifference, and which betrays extreme lack of knowledge of the nature and existence of the things which most nearly concern us, shows how little true value is to be attached to the often plausible publications by which so many deceptions as to our circumstances are nourished, and how little we can reckon upon the stability of the now existing order of things amidst the daily increasing difficulties of our times.

Thus, we saw not long since, in one of the newspapers* which are known to be edited under Catholic influence, a notice of a new measure of the Russian government, by which that barbarous power seeks to tear away, by degrees, the United Greeks (so called on account of their Rite), who have the misfortune to live under its dominion, from the communion of the Catholic Church. In this short notice the reporter, though of Catholic principles, instead of using the appropriate expression in reference to the various, but equally authorised Rites of the Catholic Church, contrasts the term United

* *Augsburger Postzeitung*, April 16, 1869. No. 89.

Greeks with the term Catholic, without the slightest mischievous intention, but without reflecting that he thereby awakens and nourishes in the public mind the false opinion that the united Greeks are, to a certain degree, defective, imperfect Catholics, a tolerated appendage, and not, in all respects, an equal portion of the Catholic Church.

Similar, sometimes more, sometimes less, important errors in expression are to be met with at every moment in these days.

Not long since, a widely circulated paper denounced, in burning words, the frivolity with which it is customary in our days to treat the action of an Œcumenical Council in defining—that is, verifying and formulising in opposition to some error—the unchangeable apostolic faith of the Catholic Church.

Nothing was wanting to these articles but the tone which should be natural to a son who grieves for the fate of the most beloved Church, our common mother, and shares her sorrows; to every one, in short, to whom these words apply—*dominicis gaudens lucris, damnis moerens,* "he rejoices over all that advances the cause of his Lord, he grieves over all that injures this holy cause." We do not hear in them the echo of that bitter sorrow which the Church felt so early, that the dirge resounds in the Lamentations of the prophet Jeremiah; that sorrow of which he expresses the true cause in the words, *Manum suam misit hostis ad omnia desiderabilia ejus, quia videt gentes ingressas sanctuarium suum, de quibus praeceperas ne intrarent in Ecclesiam tuam.* "The adversary hath spread out her hand upon all her pleasant things: for she hath seen the heathen enter into her sanctuary,"—that is, the power of the spirit of this world, "whom Thou didst command, O Lord, that they should not enter into Thy congregation"—that is, that this spirit, so opposed to Thine, should never gain influence in Thy Church.

But what is to be said when in an assembly on a religious occasion (the celebration of the jubilee of the Holy Father's ordination), a speaker, with an evident object in view, has insolently dared to say that, "if the coming Council should decree that Papal infallibility, and the opinion of the resurrection of the most blessed Virgin, and consequently of the reception of her glorified body into the mansions of bliss being already accomplished, must henceforth be accepted as dogmas, this would only be a wholesome humiliation of human pride?" Can we trust our eyes when we read such things? And is it comprehensible that no one present conceived himself bound in duty to oppose this wicked sporting with all that is most sacred, with the Faith, and with the substance of Divine Revelation?

In a time when such abnormal phenomena are possible, it is indeed necessary to rouse the faithful to watchfulness over the life of the spiritual body to which they belong, to warn them against the misconception, that they have merely to be passive recipients, that the growth of the Church is like that of inorganic matter, while it is in fact far more like that of an organism wherein a mutual action of giving and receiving is continually taking place, and where even the highest and divinely appointed authorities can give expression to nothing but that which the whole body has received from God at its first establishment, and which it guards under its true, eternal, and adorable Head.

Hence the expression, "the ancient Church," has become unadvised, inaccurate, and injurious, when it is used to separate, and so to oppose to each other the earlier and the later ages of the Church.

There is but one Holy Catholic and Apostolic Church, and this one Church extends, in its imperishable form of the new and everlasting Covenant, from the first day of Pentecost, ten days after the Ascension of the Lord, to the future consummation and fulfilment of the kingdom of God. To her is committed that substance of Divine Truth which man, by his utmost labour in the sweat of his brow, could never either create out of his own consciousness or discover by his own strength. It is committed to her for faithful, careful, loving preservation. This faith is unchangeable, as the Divine Truth of which it is a revelation. Unchangeableness is, indeed, not immobility. There can and must be a growth in richness of understanding. No limits must be placed to the deepening of the mental apprehension, to the increase of the inner life of grace. What however has not always been a dogma can never become one; this is the touchstone of Catholic truth. It must be testified by every one, as, for example, could and did happen with regard to infant baptism, when doubts respecting it arose in a respectable quarter, that it is inherent in the nature of the revealed truth relative to it, and has been expressed in the undoubted tradition of the Church respecting it. The same thing occurred with regard to the extraordinary minister of this sacrament.* Latent dogmas, that is, dogmas

* [The author refers to the duty of lay baptism in cases of necessity.—Tr.]

which have been expressly denied to be such for eighteen hundred years, and which even those who have contended for them most earnestly, as opinions, have confessed could never have authority as dogmas, such dogmas are inconceivable, because their acceptance as such would be in the most direct opposition to the true conception of the nature of the Catholic Church, and of the nature and method of her activity and operations.

Every Catholic theological work of authority bears witness to this.

It is melancholy to observe that the religious utterances of these latter days betray a view whose dead formalism is entirely opposed to the true Catholic view sketched above. We miss the pure religious warmth and heartiness which we remember in days quite gone by, and which compelled the respect even of unbelievers, and of enemies who were prejudiced against every thing Catholic, and won from them such manifold testimonies. That true and pure religious warmth made such formalism almost impossible.

This formalism may be partly owing to the unhappy political chaos of our times, and be called forth in defence against the fury and perfidy which have assumed such a form and activity, that weapons are forced into the hands even of the most peaceable.

It must, however, be partly laid to the charge of a real decay in the right method of religious instruction. Less light and warmth must be kindled by the later manner of teaching. And, in fact, we cannot doubt of it, when we look around us, and see how instruction is imparted to youths and adults in our days. The results are what might be anticipated.

The wider the spread of unbelief, and of the coarsest materialism, the more pressingly are we reminded of the sacred duty of not letting our hands be idle. "Necessity is laid upon us." Every one must put his hand to the work in order that, with

God's help, ruin may be averted. Into every family the frightful pestilence makes its way. The children, scarcely of age, forsake the path of faith which their parents still tread. Every man is robbed of his dear ones entrusted to him by God, or is threatened with the most bitter sorrow of having to look forward to appearing before the judgment-seat without those who, by nature, are his dearest treasures, and whom, in the higher order of God's providence, he has learned to esteem as the most costly pledges confided to his care.

There is no remedy for this but faithful labour, next after earnest prayer, to spread abroad a deeper and truer knowledge. In the present fateful moment we would gladly, with God's help, bring our contribution to this work in the following treatise. May the Divine Blessing not be withheld from our endeavour.

May the most reverend bishops, and likewise the whole reverend body of the clergy, lend a favourable ear to our modest treatise, and if the following propositions, however inadequately stated, meet their approval, may our fellow-Christians rectify their views of ecclesiastical affairs, and of their own relations to them, by their guidance.

And should we prove useful but to a few, to a single family, or a single soul only, we hope our reward will not be lost. For of what immeasurably greater value is a single human soul, for which the God-man has lived in the form of a servant, suffered, and shed His blood, than is the whole material universe in all the greatness and splendour by which it makes known its Creator!

I

THE Church is a living organism. She is so compacted together under her true and eternal Head, Jesus Christ, our Lord and Saviour, that, while in those of her members who have been found faithful to the end, and are now perfected in their essentially immortal part, she has already attained her end and the substance of the prize of victory, in her militant members she is still striving for the same prize; while her exclusively suffering members are healed amidst purifying pains of their wounds received in the conflict for the crown of life, and which, during its continuance, the enemy within and the world of evil spirits without keep open, or rather continually inflict anew, so that perfect healing can never be accomplished on this side the grave, or the expiation due to the perfect holiness of God be fully accomplished.

In its fulness, this organism, as the kingdom of God, includes the world of happy spirits, as is beautifully explained by St Augustine (*Enchirid.*, c. 56), and proved by Eph. iii. 15.

But, in a narrower sense, this organism is limited to the human race, whose distinctive attribute is the union of the spiritual and the material nature, or rather to that portion of mankind who acknowledge and worship in Jesus Christ not only their Creator, King, Lord, and Giver of Bliss, but also, in thankful love, their Redeemer and Saviour from the destruction they have incurred by sin.

Here we have only to inquire into what concerns the militant part of this great organism.

What constitution has her true and eternal Head given to this His Church for the term of her life here below?

We open the Holy Scriptures of the New Testament, for the subject here treated of is the Church of the New, the Everlasting Covenant, the Church of which we acknowledge, in the confession of our faith during the celebration of the Holy Mysteries, that we believe in One, Holy, Catholic, (destined to embrace all,) and Apostolic Church.

We find there the Prayer of our Lord as High Priest (John xvii.) We find what the Lord has promised to the Church, according to various places in the Holy Scriptures, as regards His intimate union with her, His presence, and the ministration of the Holy Spirit in her and through her. We find in the Apostolic Epistles (1 Cor. xii.; Eph. ii. and iv., &c.) the most exalted descriptions of this sacred organism, and of its life, as it is exhibited in time, and perfected in eternity. We find the same thing intimated in the most ancient creed, or Confession of Faith, and in more richly developed expression in the Nicene Creed; which we have just quoted. We find it further developed in the broad stream of tradition in the Church, that is, in the testimony to her belief in all epochs and periods of her existence. There, to name only some, few in number, but of characteristic significance, and of the greatest weight, we meet with the great St Ignatius; St Irenæus, in his third book against Heresies (cap. 3, 4, 24, &c.); St Cyprian, who holds a no less important position in this question, by what he has himself wrought and attested, than by the testimony his very errors have given occasion to; St Athanasius, and St Augustine. *Corpus Christi*, says this last on the 37th Psalm, *est Sancta Ecclesia, &c.*: "The body of Christ is the Holy Church dispersed throughout the world, and we belong to this body, in so far as our belief in her is pure and sincere, our hope well grounded, our love enlightened and ardent." That, to wit, is the measure of the vitality, and consequently of the durability and intimateness of our relationship to the body. And thus the testimony is carried on through all time, down to our own days. We shall have occasion to note it again and again.

And now let us look for the definitions given us by the elementary manuals, both catechisms and those composed for theologians.

On referring to the scientific compendiums of theology, we find in no one of them of any authority, published since the Church was warned by the religious revolution in the latter half of the sixteenth century, any other than that which, in substance, is comprehended in the following words: "The Church militant, or the Church in this world, is the whole society of baptized Christians, living here on earth, founded and established by Christ the Lord, and bound together by the inner bond of faith and love, and by the outward bond of profession and Church communion (*communicatio in sacris*) under the spiritual guidance and government of lawful pastors, of whom the first in rank is the successor of St Peter, whom we therefore call, by way of pre-eminence, the Pope." (*Cœtus hominum viatorum bap-*

tizatorum a Christo Domino institutus et fundatus, tum internis fidei et charitatis, tum externis professionis fidei et communionis Catholicæ vinculis colligatus, sub regimine legitimorum Pastorum, quorum primus est D. Petri successor.)

With regard to catechisms, many very indifferent ones have been in existence for a long time, though scarcely any so extremely defective as those we meet with now-a-days; but in former times too, and even until quite lately, they were also of very various degrees of merit, and some of them excellent.

We meet in one of the excellent catechisms with which the Church of France has abounded from the days of her great and glorious past, down to our own time, with these questions :—

"*Question.* In what consisted the counsel of God in the work of our redemption ?

"*Answer.* The counsel of God consisted in His forming for Himself a godly and righteous people, who should do to Him due and acceptable service.

"*Question.* What is this people ?

"*Answer.* This people is the Church. For the Church is the spiritual body of Christ. Christ is the Head of this Body. He is the Head 'from whom the whole body, fitly joined together and compacted by that which every joint supplieth, according to the effectual working in the measure of every part, maketh increase of the body unto the edifying of itself in love,' (Eph. iv. 16); and consequently, the wicked are to the spiritual body of Christ in this life, only what evil juices and diseased members are to the natural body."

And in another thoroughly excellent catechism, approved both in France and Italy, and sanctioned in Italy as late as the years 1776 and 1777, we find this question,—

"*Question.* What is the Church in the most general and comprehensive sense of the word?

"*Answer.* The Church is the society of all believers and of all the just in all ages, who form one and the same body, whose eternal, true, and proper Head is Jesus Christ, and whose soul is the Holy Spirit."

It then goes on to treat, in short, clearly arranged questions and answers of our first parents, before and after the Fall; of the faithful and confessors of the old world and of the old Covenant; of the triumphant, the suffering, and the militant Church, as the different conditions, and as it were divisions, of the one Church; and of the reasons for the designation of the Church in this life as militant. Then it continues (Part I., chap. iii., sec. 10),—

"*Question.* What is the Church, considered in its state here on earth ?

"*Answer.* In its present state, the Church is the whole society of the faithful, which, under the spiritual guidance and government of lawful pastors, endowed with the representative priesthood of Jesus Christ, forms but one and the same spiritual body, whose real and invisible Head is Jesus Christ, while her visible and ministerial chief* is the

---

* This is the admirably exact expression of the French original, and of French theological language in general, *chef ministériel.*

Roman Bishop, wherefore he is to be regarded in this capacity as the representative of Jesus Christ."

After some further questions upon the origin and nature of the Church of the New Covenant, that is, the Catholic Church, follows—

"*Question.* What meanest thou by lawful pastors ?

"*Answer.* I mean the bishops and priests who are the successors, through an unbroken series, of the apostles and first disciples of our Lord Jesus Christ, to whose authority they have succeeded (*succédent à l'autorité des Apôtres et des premiers disciples de Jésus Christ.*)"

Then follow most excellent instructions upon the body and upon the soul of the Church, upon what

The Pope is not only chief of the Church Militant in the manner in which a servant (minister) represents his Master, but he is so likewise, inasmuch as he is the first, the president of the entire episcopate and ministry of the Church, and hence the centre of sacerdotal unity. But as by the side of St Peter, St Paul appears in a pre-eminent position, so the Lord raises up in His Church from time to time extraordinary men as His instruments, each of whom He makes, as the special circumstances of the time require, a centre of doctrinal unity. Thus it was with St Athanasius, and thus it has been with many others since his time.

belongs only to the one, and upon what belongs to both, upon the distinguishing marks and prerogatives of the Church, together with all that is connected with them, (for example, the infallibility of the Church, wherein it consists, what it relates to, how it is ascertained, the two modes in which the Church, assembled or dispersed, comes to a decision in matters concerning the treasure of supernatural divine revelation confided to her, and what attitude the faithful ought to maintain previous to an undoubted decision of the Church with regard to questions which are subjects of controversy in her bosom,) upon the communion of saints, the forgiveness of sins, and the duties of the faithful towards the Church, our Mother.

What, alas! has become of this light and warmth-giving instruction, particularly within the last fifteen or twenty years?

Let us say it in a few words. In the pretended interest of the Primacy, what is its true glory, the interest of the Episcopate, has been allowed to be swallowed up in the opinion of the Christian community, who are less instructed in religion than they ever have been since the dark days of the sixteenth century. Yes, it is questionable whether, even at that time, religious instruction was so thoroughly defective, as we now, with the greatest pain, find it to be. And yet the Primacy is limited by the Episcopate, not the latter by the former, and its importance and greatness has its roots solely in the importance and greatness of the Episcopate, as has been so finely shown by the holy Pope, Gregory the Great. It is by no means a matter of indifference that the Christian community should entertain incorrect opinions on this point. It is rather in this sad state of things precisely, that the cause is to be looked for of the continually declining life of the Church, for, in Christianity especially, true light and true life are inseparable, so that injury to the one has its necessary consequence in injury to the other. An obscured light of divine truth allows as little of the growth of a thoroughly upright and consistent life, as a life cankered by pride, and generally an unholy life, can be permanently united and reconciled with a true light.

Although the Christian, the Catholic Christian community in our days may strive still to hold fast the historic faith, and in its better members may be, and in some cases undoubtedly is, endeavouring by the grace of God to attain to a living faith, or to remain stedfast and to grow therein, from want of religious knowledge, it scarcely ever, alas, attains to a clear consciousness of how inexcusably defective is its comprehension of the treasure of true religion, and how loose is the coherence of its life with the life of the whole Church.

The less the Christian community attains to this consciousness, and the more it remains a stranger to every feeling on the subject, the greater is the danger.

Christians can feel no warm interest in the empty shadow which has been imposed upon them in the place of the living and quickening idea of the Catholic Church.

The writer of these lines knows that, if in the hard-fought religious struggles of his youth no other representation of the Church had come before him, he must have fallen irretrievably into heresy and subjectivity; and he also knows that, in the like case, many others would have shared the same fate, and just those too who were in earnest about their salvation.

What does this shadow, which has succeeded in substituting itself in the place of the living idea of the Church, offer to the believer? At best—even if it rested upon truth—it would offer to the individual the means of assuring himself of the possession of religious truth in the easiest and most purely mechanical manner, of being able to verify at any given moment whether his religious thought kept pace exactly with the orthodox standard.

Thus he is only too easily brought, first to

feel obscurely, and at last, when assailed in every imaginable form by temptations from within and from without, by the mockery and scorn of the world, to cry out, What is Hecuba to me? He comes to consider the Church as an institution which he is at liberty to criticise as if he were a stranger to her; he is ever less and less at his ease in her, and, at last, he is wholly separated from her, although, as most often happens, he does not think it worth his while, or refrains through worldly reasons, from making it known.

The Catholic, on the contrary, who has gained the true idea of the Church, is inseparably united to her—so far as sin has not killed faith within him. He knows what the Church is. No disfigurement or obscuration within her can cause him any perplexity with regard to her. He feels her sufferings; they are his own. Even if human tyranny within her should threaten him with the worst, with sufferings which to a Christian mind are harder than any bodily sufferings, with the unjust infliction of those extreme spiritual penalties which were entrusted to her use by her Divine Head for the sole purpose of animating and preserving, not of killing, he says with David, when persecuted by Saul, *Si Dominus incitat te adversum me, odoretur sacrificium : si autem filii hominum, maledicti sunt in conspectu Domini, qui ejecerunt me hodie, ut non habitem in haereditate Domini, dicentes, 'Vade, servi diis alienis.'* "If the Lord have stirred thee up against me, let him accept an offering: but if they be the children of men, cursed are they before the Lord; for they have driven me out this day from abiding in the inheritance of the Lord, saying, Go, serve other Gods." (1 Sam. xxvi. 19.) Never does such a Catholic suffer himself to be tempted to evil by this heartless challenge, but he behaves in the manner described so impressively and in so few words by St Augustine in his little work, *De Verâ*

Religione, cap. iv.* Church history presents many examples of this truly Catholic conduct, but never of a time when the true doctrine of the Church, her nature and divine constitution, has experienced so serious an obscuration as we see in our days, not only carried to excess by individuals, but overspreading the Church more

---

* The passage runs thus: "Divine Providence often permits even good men to be driven out of the Catholic community by dissensions caused by carnally-minded persons. Let them bear this disgrace or this injustice with the greatest patience, in order, as far as in them lies, not to disturb the peace of the Church; let them introduce no novelties either of schism or false doctrine, and thus they will teach men by example with what hearty sincerity and purity of love we must serve God. And it is the mission of such men, either to return when the storm is allayed, or, (if that is forbidden them, either because the storm still lasts, or in order that no new and still more violent one may arise,) to benefit those very persons to whose tumult and disorder they give place, and without forming any private school, and far removed from all schism and disunion, to defend to the death, and to prove by their testimony, the faith which they are sure is that which the Catholic Church confesses. Such the Father, who seeth in secret, crowns in secret. (Matt. vi. 18.) The case is not common, yet examples are not altogether wanting, and indeed are more frequent than would be supposed." So far St Augustine in the place cited.

generally than ever before in the extravagant exaggerations occasioned by the deplorable influence of the circumstances of the times upon the affairs of the Church.

II

WHAT then is the prerogative, as compared with every other society, which the Catholic Church has received from her Divine Head, through the apostles, for the pure preservation of the true faith? It cannot be expressed better than in the words of Möhler in his *Symbolik*, (chapter v., § 38, pp. 362-364; edition of 1835). It is there shown that the earthly Church as regards the infallibility of her interpretation of the Divine Word, in respect only to what is necessary for the attainment of everlasting life, the true and genuine contents of supernatural revelation, that which we are to believe for our souls' health—has this prerogative only, that, as a divine institution, extending from time to eternity, she can never lose that capacity of life which must be utterly lost to every society before "the living thread breaks which unites the present with the past, so that henceforth all united action is impossible. All falls into confusion, the common principle is lost, amidst struggles and disputes, or disputes are even exulted in as signs of life, so that the society, whatever it may be, is undoubtedly near its dissolution, and its proper principle of growth is already paralysed. But the infallibility of the Church is modelled on the type common to all societies which are capable of life, and are therefore able to discover with certainty, and consequently cast out, when necessary, whatever is injurious to their vital principle. Accordingly, all dogmatic and moral developments which can be considered as results of a formal universal action of the Church, must be reverenced as utterances of Christ himself, and His spirit dwells in them."

We see that Möhler, as was to be expected of

him, maintains the same principle as the whole body of the fathers, without a single exception, and all great and authoritative Catholic theologians of all ages, viz., that when we speak of infallible decrees in matters of faith, those only can be meant which may be looked upon as the results of a formal universal action of the Church. Hence it is, that the noble convert, Count Stolberg, in his translation of two short works of St Augustine, in the last note (pp. 348, 349), complains that the Catholic Church is calumniated by a respectable Protestant theologian in the then new *Berliner Monatsschrift* of 1801, as though she acknowledged a visible head endued with power to prescribe dogmas, and believed in the infallibility of the Pope.

In the conference, or religious colloquy, of Bossuet, with Claude, the Protestant theologian, the principle taught by Möhler is established with irresistible power by that great bishop and teacher of these later times. In this conference the subject treated of is exclusively the Church, and the meaning of belief in the Church in the Apostles' creed and the Nicene. At the critical point where Claude urges that, if the Catholic doctrine of the Church were true, the authority of the synagogue would have made the rejection of our Saviour both lawful and obligatory; and where that great, in almost all respects unsurpassed, and model teacher and champion of the Catholic Church,* lifts up his heart to God in prayer that he would enable him to make plain to the listeners (who, without exception, were all Protestants), the shameful untruth of this insidious fallacy, and then with all the irresistible power of truth proceeds to show, that at all times an infallible living authority in matters of faith has existed and will exist in this world, whereby it is recognised, and how it acts,—it does not occur to him, in the most distant manner, any more than in any of his writings or in those of any Catholic controversialist of the slightest reputation, even to

* See Appendix.

mention Papal infallibility as a possibility, or hypothesis only.

These great men knew too well that God's ways are otherwise ordered, that a principle of life proceeds from Him, which has to obtain the mastery, not only over the actions and inclinations, but over the understanding, often through hard struggles, from which there would be indeed a very easy escape, if the opinion of the Pope's infallibility when speaking *ex cathedrâ*,—and the conditions of this *ex cathedrâ* decision must also be formulized,—were the expression of a divine ordinance.

Bossuet adopts in this conference the expression used by Claude, that the Apostles were "auteurs de la révélation," *i.e.*, original organs of divine revelation, while the Church can only lay claim to the right interpretation thereof, and he then explains how the Church is protected and guided in this interpretation by the Holy Spirit in the same manner as they were guided and protected by the same Holy Spirit in the first promulgation and formulizing of the contents of revelation.

In this work, which is incumbent upon the Church, as in the justification and sanctification of each individual member of the Church, a divine action and guidance must constantly co-operate with human activity. The life of the whole Church, like the life of her individual members, consists in this divine influence on human action. It is conditional upon the exertions each individual must make, as also upon the exertions which are incumbent upon the Church in order to the fulfilment of her high office. "For the kingdom of heaven suffers violence." (Matt. xi. 12.) And it is in these efforts and struggles that the dangers exist which threaten the Church to the last. It is in consequence of these hindrances which have to be overcome, these dangers which have to be withstood, that periods of obscuration of the faith occur from time to time in her life, whereof the most dangerous, because the most complicated and the most general, is that in which we now find ourselves. It appears to bear about it, but too surely, the marks foretold by the very lips of eternal truth, in those pregnant words, "When the Son of man cometh, shall he find the faith on earth?" (Luke xviii. 8,) and, "If it were possible, they shall deceive the very elect." (Matt. xxiv. 24.) These words of our Lord, whose import has filled the saints of all ages with amazement and holy awe, find us, alas! who witness so much at least of their actual fulfilment, cold and indifferent, as if they concerned us not, and yet they alone can render comprehensible what we have lived to witness, both in the secular and religious world.

It was not only the fathers of the Church who were cognisant of these obscurations, one of the earliest of which they recognised in the long duration and tough vitality of Arianism. As early as during the progress of that heresy,

St Athanasius points out that it is by no means always the majority in the Church that has full and explicit possession of the whole truth, which forms the treasure of divine revelation confided to her. The early supporters of Curialism* were also aware of these periods of obscuration, for that system was completely formed before it was developed to the extreme point to which we have lately seen it carried for the first time—at least by its theological representatives, and those who lay claim to authority as

---

* We never use the word Ultramontanism. This appellation appears to us thoroughly inappropriate, not only because it does not describe the nature of the thing, but is borrowed from a mere accident of geographical situation, so that if the meaning of words were attended to, it would be utterly inapplicable beyond the limits of France and Northern Europe, or in the strictest sense, of Germany; and because in Italy itself, which possesses very great, very saintly, and very numerous opponents of that pernicious system, it would have to be changed into Cismontanism; but because, for the reason just mentioned, it is unjust towards Italy. We mean by Italy, only the ancient nation, not the monstrous conglomeration which it pleases the absolutism of the revolution to dress up with this name. Furthermore, this appellation, Ultramontane, which might be tolerated in places and circumstances in which it is, at least, outwardly suitable, is, in our judg-

teachers—within the last thirty-eight years, and still more within the last twenty years.

We will quote one witness in proof of this, the Cardinal Torquemada, commonly called in Latin, Turrecremata. This firm adherent of the already completely formed curialistic system, (who has indeed been left far behind by the curialists of the last hundred and fifty, or hundred years, while the supporters of the headlong curialism of the last forty or twenty years can only look upon him as a feeble beginner,) speaks thus on

ment, no longer admissible at least in Germany, in these days of religious desolation, perplexity, and confusion, when we hear it applied indifferently to the most correct and most distorted views by the enemies and slanderers of all religion, who boldly discuss and slander that of which they absolutely know nothing and will learn nothing. Hence this word Ultramontanism only increases the general mental confusion to the great hurt of religion, and, among us in Germany, of our earthly fatherland also. The word Curialism, on the contrary, describes both the nature and the seat of the evil. It is that courtier spirit, which the great St Basil detected and sharply rebuked in its first beginnings, and which has since attained a giant's growth, and is the seat of the evil—the *Curia*, the court which surrounds the Papal Chair, and exercises over it the most deplorable influence.

the subject in his *Summa de Ecclesiâ*, (lib. iii. c. 60,) "*Nunquam fides deficiet de Ecclesiâ, quoniam semper in aliquibus, multis aut paucis, fides permanebit usque in finem.*" "The faith will never cease to belong to the Church, because at all times, in some of its members, be they many, or (as at present) only a few, the faith (perfect, pure, and inviolate,) will remain and exist until the end." What Turrecremata adds in the same book, in accordance with his curialistic views, does not belong to this place, and is, as could be easily shown, in irreconcilable contradiction to this statement of the ancient truth which he had received by tradition. The comparatively new and erroneous view does not harmonise with the ancient tradition of religious truth.*

And now, let us draw nearer to the question, What is the place and organic function of the Episcopate in the Church, and especially in an Œcumenical Council?

* See also chapter lxv. of the same book of this work.

The Bishops are possessors of the fulness of the ministerial priesthood,* instituted by our Lord and Saviour Jesus Christ, to represent Him in the accomplishment of His work upon earth to the end of the world, and furnished by Him with the necessary powers; and this priesthood can be imparted and propagated by the bishops alone in the sacrament of ordination, which, like baptism and confirmation, implants an indelible character upon the soul. Hence bishops are set over simple priests in the spiritual government of the dearly purchased flock.

It follows from what has been said, that bishops are "set by the Holy Ghost to govern the Church of God." Hence we read in Acts xx. 28: "Take heed therefore unto yourselves, and to all the flock, over the which the Holy Ghost hath made you overseers, to feed the Church of God, which He hath purchased with His own blood." And again,

---

* We call it ministerial, to distinguish it from the spiritual priesthood to which every Christian is called.

"Feed the flock of God which is among you, taking the oversight thereof, not by constraint, but willingly; not for filthy lucre, but of a ready mind; neither as being lords over God's heritage, but being ensamples to the flock." (1 Peter v. 2, 3.)

It is worthy of remark that they are the princes of the apostles, Peter and Paul, who speak thus of the exalted dignity of the Bishops, and of the duties which are imposed upon them, and also of the significance and the functions of the episcopate in the Catholic Church.

Assembled around the first among them, and in co-operation with their brethren, the priests, they are set to govern the Church in the spirit of brotherly counsel.

This counsel is brought into operation in the most solemn manner when an Œcumenical Council is held.

If ever, or anywhere, it is at the time and during the sitting of such a Council that the members of the episcopal order must prove themselves, by their discharge of the functions, to be the highest and noblest divinely appointed organs of the Church.

For at no time, and on no occasion, could there be a more manifest and significant realisation of the promise made to the Church, that her Lord and head will be with her unto the end of the world, and that the Holy Spirit will lead her into all truth.

This has been proved in the most difficult circumstances, even when in such assemblies the Holy Spirit has been grieved in various ways.

But it is an indispensable condition that the Bishops should not be unfaithful to, or renounce their essential functions; they must acknowledge them, and faithfully fulfil them, at least, in giving judgment on matters of faith and on dogmatic questions.

For the privilege here treated of is so peculiarly the property of the whole Church, and is so entirely incommunicable, that a truly Œcumenical Council, that is, not only one which has been legitimately summoned, but which is legitimately conducted, can never have the power either of transferring the infallibility in matters of faith which belongs and is only promised to the whole Church, to her ministerial head, or of declaring that this infallibility equally belongs and is promised to him.

Gerson, that great luminary among the illustrious doctors of the Church, who was holy in his life and in his death, defines an Œcumenical Council, to be an assembly of the whole hierarchy of the Catholic Church, called together by lawful authority in an appointed place, without excluding any member who desires a hearing, and the object of which is, to treat of, and set in order, what concerns Church government in regard to faith and practice.

In this definition, the essential conditions are pointed out which are collectively requisite for a Council to have claims to the character of a General Council.

They are—1. The legitimacy of the summoning

power; 2. The legitimacy of the occasion of this summons; 3. The perfect fulfilment of the obligations incumbent upon them by the members of the Council, in order to enable them to attain to the truth in the controverted questions of faith under discussion, and to decide aright upon the ordinances and decrees to be published; and this condition is so indispensable, that if it be neglected, the assistance of the Holy Spirit is not promised; and, 4. in order that the perfect fulfilment of these obligations may be possible, absolute freedom of speech, of investigation, of deliberation, and of voting.

Without this thorough completeness and absolute freedom in the transactions of a Council, all its decisions are utterly null and void, and have no binding authority. And this completeness and absolute freedom must be as clear as the sun at noonday.

The curialistic system does away with the necessity and even with the use of a Council, for what it is in the power of one to do, he does better alone than with colleagues, as is abundantly proved by experience, both with regard to teaching and government. Bossuet remarks upon this, in his colloquy with Claude, and then concludes; *Ce n'est pas précisément l'intention ni l'institution des Synodes (d'instruire), car un particulier savant donnera plus d'instruction que tout un Synode ensemble. Ce qu'il faut donc attendre d'un Synode n'est pas tant l'instruction, qu'une décision par autorité,* a laquelle il faille céder; car c'est de *quoi ont besoin les ignorants qui doutent et les superbes qui contredisent.* " It is not exactly the object or the intention of a synod (to instruct), for an individual man of learning will impart more instruction than a whole synod. What is to be expected then of a synod, is not so much instruction, as an authoritative decision to which obedience must be yielded, for this is what is needed by the ignorant who doubt and by the proud who gainsay." How much soever then the curialistic doctrine is opposed to the necessity of Œcumenical Councils, in certain cases, and under certain conditions,—conditions, the absence or neglect of which, more or less deprive Councils of that character,—the supporters of this system were compelled to admit this necessity, and endeavoured to fit them on to their system as they best could, saying, as for example Suarez writes, (*De Fide*, Disp. 10), *Concilia Generalia ad generales causas et dogmata fidei definienda congregari, quam consuetudinem ab Apostolis initium habuisse, a Christo Domino mandâsse, suppositâ fide et institutione Ecclesiæ a Christo factâ ejusque gubernatione, quasi naturalis ratio dictat talium conciliorum celebrationem.* "The practice of assembling General Councils for deliberation upon the general affairs of the Church, and for the decision of questions of faith, has its origin in the direction of our Lord Jesus Christ, and in the example of His apostles; and the faith of the Church, and its institution and government by Christ being pre-supposed, one cannot but grant that nature itself and human reason appear to suggest the holding of such assemblies, it being natural to desire the advice and consent of many in weighty and serious affairs." What a miserable evasion, just for the sake of allowing the fact of the holding of Councils, and of the nature and method of their deliberations in Christian antiquity, to subsist peacefully side by side with the curialistic system! This system can urge nothing more in this direction, even if it succeeds so far. For the necessity of Œcumenical Councils is entirely done away with by this system, since, according to it, the whole authority of the decision depends solely upon the ministerial head of the Church, upon his assent or his veto, while the previous examination of the opportuneness of the decision must also be left to him.*

Were this the right way to proceed, why should a Council be held? Why give so much trouble to the chief pastors of the Church? Why withdraw, at least the greater number of them, from their usual and regular spheres of work for a considerable

---

* This principle has quite recently been most emphatically insisted upon in the Papal organ, the *Civiltà Cattolica.*—TR.

time? If merely for the information of the Pope, truly learned theologians,—and all bishops are not and need not be that, and perhaps unfortunately too few such are to be found—would be more fit for the purpose. The representation of the whole Church and of her whole hierarchy could be in no way needful.

The practice of holding Œcumenical Councils so constant, so solemn, so unanimous, in combination with the circumstances under which each was summoned, and with the nature and method of their proceedings, is alone enough to prove the entire inadmissibility of the curialistic system; and one can only wonder at the fancy of a party, now all powerful in Rome, for choosing the form of a Council for the purpose of declaring Councils to be superfluous for all future time. By this more than whimsical fancy, they bear witness against their own system. If, however, the fulness of the spiritual authority is not given to an individual, but, as is taught by all the Fathers without exception, exclusively to the whole society, it is easy to understand that the unanimous agreement of the pastors of the Church upon a point of doctrine is necessary for the passing of a decree in matters of faith, since they are the authorised exponents of her mind. It is also easy to understand that there are cases in which they require common intercourse, investigation, and impartial comparison and discussion, in order—with the assistance of the Holy Spirit, then not withheld—to arrive at a clear and safe judgment. In such a mode of action, and in no other, they are able to impart their ideas to one another, not without the co-operation of the second order of pastors, simple priests and learned theologians, as such—of whom, however, this is not the place to speak. They thus afford each other mutual help towards the great and sacred object in view, first, of throwing light upon subjects which have been more or less obscured, even among Catholics, by long and violent controversies, in order to separate genuine and ancient tradition from that which is new and spurious, and to lead minds and spirits to that agreement upon which the whole strength of a decision depends; and, secondly, in order to arrive at a clearer expression of the doubted, obscured, or controverted article of Catholic faith, of disentangling it from scholastic subtleties, and expounding it from the Holy Scriptures, and the writings of the Fathers in a manner exact, plain, and ample enough to lay bare all the windings of a dangerous error, and divide it, by the definition which has become necessary, from the sacred domain of the faith. They will then propound this clearer exposition of the unchangeable truth with the full authority of a thorough unity and genuine agreement, and thus unite all the intelligence and forces of the Church in a successful resistance to all attempts at innovation, which, in matters of faith, can only be error.

This need of mutual help, which unites men in their character of ordained instruments for the maintenance of revealed truth, and for deepening the understanding of it among men—this

THE CHURCH OF GOD AND THE BISHOPS 55

holy concord, wherein, free from all tyranny and compulsion, they have to seek knowledge of the truth, in order to maintain it inviolate—exactly agrees with the idea of the Catholic Church given us by the Fathers, and the divine intention in its institution, viz., to preserve men in humility, and to keep them united in one and the same body, so as to form a single organism, which bears witness to its Author throughout all time, and gives to Him the honour which to Him alone is due.

This is the plan which the Fifth Œcumenical Council has delineated of the constitution and action of the Catholic Church. What Bossuet says with regard to this, in the *Defensio Declarationis Cleri* (lib. xii., c. 17, 18, 20, 29, 31, 40), is also most instructive, and not less so what he says elsewhere (lib. i., c. 2; lib. iii., c. 2; lib. xii. c. 6 *sqq.*) in the same important work.*

* We may here cite Melchior Canus' work as a pendant to Bossuet's (lib. v., c. 5 and 15). This great theologian, who was a member of the Dominican Order, and the opponent of Lainez in the Council of Trent, and who afterwards became Bishop of the

What can be more excellent than the function of the episcopate as it is thus manifested to us? For what is more sublime, more sacred, more inviolable than the true faith? Not one tittle may be taken away from it, nor may one tittle be added to it. Even what we deduce, however correctly, according to the analogy of the faith, from undoubted dogmas, is not on that account alone itself a dogma or article of faith.

There is something infinitely sacred about a dogma of which the present generation can scarcely

---

Canary Islands, was, it is well known, far from being what is called a Gallican. Yet we can appeal to him almost as well as to Bossuet against the excessive curialism of the present day. He says, among other things: *Commune est, mihi crede, omnibus Ecclesiæ judicibus, ut si decreta ediderint temeritate quâdam, sine judicio, repentino quasi vento incitati, nihil omnino conficiant quod solidum, quod grave, quod certum habetur.* "Believe me, it is true of all who are placed as judges in the Church (that is, the bishops), that, when they make decisions and draw up decrees, (to whatsoever these may relate), from the impulse of a certain temerity, without ripe judgment, (that is, without a thorough previous examination), and, as it were, blown about by a sudden gust of wind, they then establish nothing well-founded, nothing solid, nothing certain."

form a just conception; the language even of the better-minded, of those who have at least good will, is so strange in regard to these questions. The devotion of the whole man, and the imperative obligations which a Christian owes to a real dogma or article of faith, are scarcely taken into account; nor is it considered how entirely incommunicable this exalted property is, and that the supreme intelligence of God alone can impose an article of faith upon the human intelligence created by Him, nor with what transparent clearness the divine revelation of every real dogma must be proved, and be capable of proof.

The office of the Bishops in an Œcumenical Council, if an assembly of the Church is really to maintain this character, is then, first as representatives of the whole Church—for *Episcopatus unus est cujus a singulis in solidum pars tenetur*[*]—to bear witness to the unchangeable confession of her faith,

---

[*] St Cyprian, *De Unitate Ecclesiæ*. "There is but one episcopate held in solidarity by each separate bishop."

and for each individual bishop to bear witness to the faith of his own diocese from the earliest times, without the least regard to his own theological system or views or particular opinions, however pious and salutary they may be, or may appear to be, both to himself and others. His living, and, in this sense, purely objective testimony must be confirmed by historical documents and vouchers. All the evidence must first be collated and compared, and any obscure points explained, during which examination a hearing must be given in full Council to the priests of the second order, and to the learned theologians among them, to Theological Faculties, and to the members of other ecclesiastical corporations, who possess well-earned rights, which, under divine providence, are most useful with regard to the historical development of religious questions,—indeed, according to Gerson, no member of the Church ought to be absolutely refused a hearing,—and then the judicial functions of the Bishops are called into action. With the same abnegation* with which it is the duty of a civil judge to look entirely away from his own view of the case before him, and to turn his eyes to the law which he has to administer,—nay, with a far purer, far stricter, far more unconditional self-renunciation,—must the Bishops who have to deal with what God has revealed, solemnly declare what has been proved to be the genuine doctrine of the Catholic Church, in respect to which we refer the reader to the exposition of the idea of the Catholic Church, given in the first part of this discussion, and remind him of the famous and well-known maxim, which can never be often enough repeated, *Quod semper, quod ubique, quod ab omnibus.*†

---

* Renunciation of, or abstinence from, personal prejudices and preferences.

† Vincent.—Lerinensis *Commonitorium.* "That only is an essential part of the Catholic faith which has always, everywhere, (in the Catholic Church), and by all, been faithfully believed and confessed." This threefold criterion St Vincent carries further and says : "We must never swerve from these articles of faith," (either by diminution, we would add, or by multiplication or enlarge-

Never must the Bishops forget, if the Council is to possess and maintain to the end an Œcumenical character, that in their capacity of judges of the faith, they are only judges, and not in the slightest degree lawgivers, or creators. While, in virtue of their delegation by the true shepherd and bishop of our souls, they have certainly, according to the analogy of the faith, an initiative and administrative legislative authority to be wisely used, in what belongs to the government of the earthly Church, for the furtherance and accomplishment of the great task laid upon it, and with a view to its varying circumstances; in respect to dogma, not the shadow

---

ment), "of which it is evident and notorious that they have been believed and confessed by our fathers in the faith, and our predecessors in the Catholic profession. And if an innovation appears to be taking hold, no longer merely on a greater or lesser part, but almost on the whole Church, and disturbing the security of her children's faith, what is then the duty of the true and blameless Catholic Christian? He must take good heed to hold fast to Christian antiquity, and to guide himself by its creed, for that blessed antiquity can no longer be led astray by any deceitful innovation which makes bold to pretend to be the ancient and genuine Catholic faith."

of such authority belongs to them. Even in the Holy Council of Trent, the proceedings were not always, and in all points, in accordance with the ever authoritative examples of Christian antiquity, and therefore, not always free from blame, as has already been sufficiently explained. A still further modernisation of the mode of proceeding would only cause the most serious doubts to be entertained of the possibility of any future Council possessing an Œcumenical character.

There must be no question of a mode of proceeding by which measures are arranged and prepared beforehand by packed committees, however honourable they may be, so that nothing is left to the Bishops but to inspect what is already cut out for them, with a highly problematical influence upon the final revision.

There must be no question of a mode of proceeding, by which the depositions of witnesses, and the discussions upon them, are to be, as it were, pre-supposed, and the Bishops are to subscribe, merely on the ground of the documents laid before them, what is substantially a pre-arranged system, as if it were their own unanimous judgment.

There must be no question of a Council in which Bishops have a vote and seat by favour only, or where priests, not to speak of well-intentioned laymen,* can appear and obtain 'a hearing by favour only. A council of this character would be no Œcumenical Council.

Lastly, what took place in Rome in the year 1854, must not, in the most remote degree, be taken as an example of the method of proceeding.

It is, therefore, our deliberate opinion that although, under less abnormal circumstances than prevail at present, a Council would be of the greatest use to the Church, and indeed, were the times not so extraordinarily bad, would be necessary for the settlement of internal questions pending in the Church for about the last 250

* *See* La Gerson, *De Potest. Eccles.* Cons. 12.

years, yet, to undertake to hold one now can only be considered as in the highest degree hazardous.

There are, indeed, tasks in abundance to occupy an Œcumenical Council. There is need of a plain exposition of the true genius of Christianity in accordance with the wants of the age, and of the notes of that true righteousness to which we Christians are called. There is need to put an end to the lethargic ignorance of the nations, both of the true and pure teaching of the Church and of the Holy Scriptures. There is need to oppose the opinion that mere attrition is sufficient to the holy sacrament of penance, with all that depends upon it, and the practical denial it involves of the indispensable commandment of love towards God, whereby the whole Divine Law is disfigured, and that extreme monstrosity made possible, which is only too well known under the name of Probabilism.* There is need to confirm afresh, and to

* The Jesuit system of casuistry.—Tr.

prescribe in the strictest manner, the rules for the administration of the holy sacrament of penance, inclusive of the urgently required regulation of the very weighty matter of the Easter communion —seizing the opportunity of settling the extremely important question of what constitutes the sin of usury, in a sense far removed from that wholly inadmissible laxity which has crept in in this important matter, and from well-meant mistakes, as well as, still more, from Pharisaic views and practice. Thus the Church would be enabled to assist powerfully in stopping one of the main sources of the otherwise irremediable increase of that shocking modern pauperism which proceeds mainly from four causes : viz., usury ;* the change of trade into gambling, which anticipates the profits of labour as winnings; love of pleasure; and luxury. There is need of a reformátion in

---

* The nature of usury consists in becoming richer by mere lending, and, as well as gaming, is forbidden by the law of God. Lotteries are included in this condemnation.

the government of the Church in conformity with a clearer and more correct teaching of her nature and constitution. There is need of a regulation of the relations between Church and State,* so far as this is required by the various political constitutions, whereby the canonical election of bishops and all other corresponding ecclesiastical arrangements might be restored. There is need of explanation and rectification of the doctrine and practice of indulgences, as also in regard to marriage and the holy sacrament of marriage, dispensations of all kinds, the fitting conduct of the Church with regard to really dangerous books, but only what are really such, and the proceedings to be accordingly taken against them in every diocese and province, at the instance of the ecclesiastical authorities. Regulations for the liturgy are also needed, to put an end, as is earnestly desired by all judicious persons, to the Vandalism and the wholly un-catholic thirst for uniformity which

* See Second Appendix.

have crept in with the thoroughly modern spirit of universal centralisation and its bureaucratism,* and, in connection with this, directions about

* The Church of France, from which, in former days, when curialism was unknown, the Church of Rome borrowed much, was in possession of the most valuable liturgical treasures and peculiarities, and of these last, there are venerable and important examples in almost all the great national Churches which are portions of the whole Catholic Church. If what is said above is applicable to Missals and Rituals, it is far more so to the office of the Church, which forms the obligatory manual for the devotions of the clergy and regulars, whether said singly, or in common, and which, in the form of the present Roman Breviary, has become an unprofitable burden for the generality. How excellent, on the contrary, are the breviaries of the French Church! What an enlightened arrangement of the psalms! What wise rules with regard to the ferial offices, the *Proprium Sanctorum*, and the (seldom used) *Commune* of various kinds. Every one of these is admirable, which cannot be said of any *Commune* of the Roman Breviary. What glorious hymns, while too many of the Roman Breviary hymns are in every respect beneath all criticism! What an admirably practical and compact course of "*Theologia mentis et cordis*" he who uses one of these breviaries goes through annually, while the Roman Breviary retains only the wreck of it! What an absence of all that is legendary and unworthy of being offered to the God of truth! What a perfect arrangement of the offices for every feria, of which no notice is taken in the Roman Breviary, although this ecclesiastical name for the days of the week expresses in Latin that the whole life of a Christian should be a foretaste of heaven. Even Sundays, with the exception of some

Church music and chanting drawn up at once with scientific and artistic knowledge and in an ecclesi-

few privileged days, are ignored in the present Roman use, and have to give way on every occasion, without considering that the excellent old Roman sequence of Sundays is thus destroyed, with the instruction conveyed by them to the people. What a rich store of collects in the Church of France, and how familiar were the people formerly with the offices of the Church, with that *lex supplicandi* which gives the rule for the *lex credendi!* How many laymen even prayed from the Breviary either in the language of the Church or in their mother tongue! For provision was made for all. And while this example ought to be followed in all countries, restored and maintained in France itself, curialistic and Jesuitic Vandalism are destroying what is still extant there, and the like of which is nowhere to be revived. The people have to remain strangers to the Divine Office, and are fed upon defective, and often paltry prayer-books, and with the rosary, which is a venerable kind of meditative prayer, and for that very reason wholly unfit to be almost the only popular form of devotion, and especially unfit to be screamed aloud as is usually done, when it can only cause pain or even anger to every unprejudiced hearer, and furnish the world with an occasion for scoffing. We can only lament most deeply that besides all this, for some years past, the best recommendation of a foreign prelate in Rome is, that he sweeps away, as quickly as possible, all usages and customs, however good, and all historical recollections, not in order to restore unity, which does not require such a Vandalism of uniformity, but to produce a dead uniformity and similarity down to the minutest particular, which savours, not of the spirit of the Catholic Church, but of the barrack.

astical spirit. An examination and reform should be prescribed of the catechisms which have become so incredibly bad almost everywhere of late;* a reform of the process of canonisation, and in the preparation for entrance into the clerical profession, but not in a spirit hostile to the Theological Faculties in the universities, which could only lead to the most deplorable maiming of the Church, since reason and experience teach us that a learned clergy is absolutely necessary for the full development of

---

* The poorest catechisms which were in use in Germany twenty years ago, if they did not promote, at least did not overthrow the right understanding of the faith and the nature of the Church, and did not make it impossible; they at least left room for it. What belonged to the beginning stood at the beginning, and what concerned the end found its corresponding place at the end of the catechism. If the questions were not always, in a psychological and educational sense, rightly arranged, and were often wanting in a deep and living comprehension of the most sacred substance of the faith, and thus failed to illustrate its strength, power, and excellence, yet subjects were not wantonly distorted, and, in common phrase, turned upside down. In short, there was poverty, sometimes great poverty to be deplored, but one had not then to deal with disfigurements, or with unseemly superfluities and amplifications. The catechist could infuse a soul into the imperfect form, and, as through an unclosed well, draw treasures of life from the deep.

her strength in the ordinary course of things. A restoration is needed of the true religious life, which is in fact, as the marrow in the bones, silent but necessary for strength, and when it proceeds from, and is guided by a right and enlightened spirit, can manifest itself in accordance with the exigencies of the times, in the most admirable external activity. There is also need for the arrangement of several other important affairs of the Church, for which an appeal

We speak of this from experience. Since the victory of curialism everything is changed. In the catechisms now in use—we can point out examples if required—principles and consequences, the end and the means, are so jumbled together, that it is impossible to gain from them a complete view of the faith, in respect to doctrine and life. The best catechist can do nothing with them; at the utmost he can only diminish the evil. And all this is in consequence of the un-catholic but curialistic view of the Church now prevailing, with its undue exaltation of the primacy, which it would convert into an autocracy. So true it is that this system, subversive of the true idea of the Catholic Church and incompatible with its true constitution and life, which does away with the idea, strength and power, and very essence of the Church, as completely as Scholasticism (the perverse scholastic divinity) does away with the idea, strength and power, and the essence of the Faith, and which threatens to rob us by degrees of all we value, is absolutely incompatible with a living and fruitful system of instruction.

has long been made to the highest ecclesiastical judgment-seat on earth, to a lawful Œcumenical Council which shall establish and maintain its character as such.

What immense tasks! For almost every one of these questions falls into several subdivisions on which we cannot dwell here. It is evident, that without thinking of dogmatic definitions in the proper sense of the word, for which the present time does not offer even an occasion, far less an opportunity, to say nothing of a necessity, what remains to be achieved is only too difficult.

We need not dwell longer on this subject, or indicate more precisely the matters we have only just touched upon, because it is our painful conviction that the circumstances of the Church at this unhappy period are not such as to lead us to hope for a more salutary treatment in a Council than they have lately experienced singly. As Savigny denied that the deeply distempered times were fit for civil legislation—we were lately reminded of it by an excellent man whom we have learned to value—we must do the same in ecclesiastical affairs, having regard to the still more disordered condition of the Church, which is the same as is described by the holy Pope, Gregory the Great, in the words: *Quum in diebus illis Ecclesia, quasi quodam senio debilitata, per prædicationem filios parere non valet, reminiscitur fœcunditatis antiquæ.* "In days to come, the Church, enfeebled as it were by old age, and unable as formerly to increase the number and excellence of her children by the promulgation of the Divine Word, will look back with regret on the days of her former fruitfulness," &c.*

For what a diametrically opposite view of the Church now prevails. According to it the Pope is an absolute monarch—only vice-monarch, of course, but still the true monarch is often scarcely mentioned,†—and the remainder of the bishops, or rather

* *Moral.* in cap. 29 Job, cap. 12.
† Or mention is made of Him in a manner most unworthy of Him, and exactly reversing the true relations. We find in the Harbéschen Catechism, p. 18, Q. "What is the Church?" A.

the bishops, are his vicars, or representatives, his delegates, the chief presidents whom this monarch has set over the provinces of his empire. They receive his commands, plainly so called, and without any further reserve, both in the place whence they issue and in the place where they are received, however little this expression agrees with the words of our Saviour (Luke xxii. 25-27) and several other places, with those of the holy Apostle, Peter (1 Peter vi. 1-4) and with the whole history of the Church. And the Bishops who receive these commands obey them unconditionally, or if not, they are "regulated" in every possible manner; nay the ideal striven after is that they shall be deposed without further ceremony, or *de facto* superseded by a so-called co-adjutor, who would only leave to them the name of the exalted stewardship to which they have been

"The Church is the great visible community of all Christians upon earth, who under their common supreme head, the Pope of Rome," &c. Q. "Is not Christ the supreme Head of the Church?" A. Christ is indeed the Head of the Church, but the invisible Head!" —How perversely this is stated!

called by the Holy Ghost; while, on the other hand, these Bishops on their part are at liberty to deal, and in fact do, deal in the same manner with the inferior clergy, that is, the priests of the second order, their companions in their unspeakably great office of representatives of the Lord, and with the deacons and clerks of the lower orders, except where a priest is to be supported against his —perhaps not sufficiently blindly and unconditionally obedient—Bishop, and is to be given a triumph over him by way of warning to others. It is significant that a report has been lately spread that the revolutionary measure was to be everywhere introduced of making the parish priest *amovibilis ad nutum*. As the Italians say, *Se non é vero, é ben trovato*. If it is not true, it is well imagined, and quite in the spirit of those of whom we have been speaking. Amidst such formalism and bureaucratism, against which the hatred of municipal and political society, continually sinking deeper in materialism and unbelief, wages an inveterate war on its own behalf, and with its own detestable weapons, ecclesiastical affairs have fallen into a state which may be understood from our enumeration of the true duties of an Œcumenical Council; and the Church, Religion, and the only true and durable morality lose ground daily.*

A complete autocracy has in fact been substituted for the constitution which our Lord gave to His Church, and if the expressions which have been handed down to us by a sacred antiquity are still in use, their spirit is no longer in force. The title still remains, "Servant of the servants of God," but alas! we are thus involuntarily reminded of the emphasis with which, for example, a Frederick II. of Prussia called himself the servant of the state, by which was understood in the minds of his

---

* We cannot enter here into a discussion of the nature, causes, and significance of the successes obtained in England and America, which stand in apparent contrast with the phenomena visible elsewhere. It would, however, be easy to analyse them, and to prove this appearance of a contrast with the general phenomena to be a delusion, however much we, too, as faithful children of the Church, thank God that so many individuals are thus led into the way of life.

servants, and gradually in those of his people, no less than in his own, that he himself was the state, quite in the spirit of the words ascribed to Louis XIV., *L'état c'est moi.* "I am the state."

In temporal governments this exaggeration of the monarchical principle—which within due limits is certainly the best for civil constitutions, which are not, like that of the Church, of immediate divine institution—has led to the precisely opposite extreme.

In ecclesiastical government we do not indeed see that the exaggeration of the monarchical principle, which we have faithfully described, has as yet produced the opposite extreme in those populations and portions of populations of the Catholic confession who do not wish to break with the faith, to whom religious faith is still a necessity, and who, accepting that which, alas! is alone offered to them, pay homage to this exaggeration, which, in the Church, is more than an exaggeration; it is a deformation of its true constitution. Rather does the excessive and repulsive impiety which is seen on all sides excite at present the still existing though unenlightened piety of believers to manifestations equally excessive in their kind, to expressions and evtravagances which show that at least the greater number mean to do, and believe they do, something quite different from what they really effect. But let no one deceive himself in this fatal manner. Nothing but the truth, the full, pure, strengthening truth, fostered in the spirit of love, will be able to meet the coming storm; for, as St Augustine inculcates, "In passing through life, we can only enter into divine truth by love."*

---

* The curialism of the present time is so excessive and extravagant, that the followers of this system who lived in days not long gone by, must have been filled with alarm could they have witnessed it. The truly pious among them, like Cardinal Pacca, and the worldly wise, like Cardinal Consalvi, would scarcely know whether they were waking or dreaming. What the holy Pope, Gregory the Great, would say on the subject need not be dwelt upon. The contrast would be too painfully striking. Bishops who are summoned to obey without murmuring in a manner which, in temporal matters, is only required, and consequently, only borne for the sake of military discipline, are phenomena of

THE CHURCH OF GOD AND THE BISHOPS 77

We have only been able, at this critical moment, with a heart filled with sorrow, to touch slightly and superficially upon the weighty subject on which so much depends. We acknowledge and feel only too deeply that it has been done in an imperfect form. There is, however, one more point to which we would draw attention in concluding this fragmentary discussion.

which there have been hitherto no examples in the Church;—in the Church wherein, even when obedience is to be the rule in the strictest sense of the word (which cannot be rigidly the case in the relations between the other bishops and the Pope), it is, and is always to be, only an intelligent obedience, based on deliberation and understanding, except in very rare cases of the higher ascetic life, which belong to the direction of individual souls, and must not be confounded with the general administration of the Church of God. All reliable Catholic theologians are unanimous in declaring and proving that the maxims of obedience, inculcated by the Society of Loyola, are an immoderate exaggeration, carried to caricature, of the maxims relative to this duty taught by the true and genuine masters of the inner life. It is remarkable that the so-called Jesuits are only guilty of this exaggeration of the ascetic life in one respect, while in all else they maintain the principle of laxity. But to return to the government of the Church, it is evident that in ruling it, according to the views of the above-named society, the αἴρεσις δεσποτείας—Bossuet's *Heresie de la Domination*—has already reached its extreme point.

How can any one believe, when the whole undertaking with all the apparatus relating to it is, as is too conspicuous, forced upon the Holy Father—how can any one indulge the delusive hope that Oriental schismatics and Protestants will be won over by it?

Protestantism, in the mass, has indeed wandered so far from all churchmanship and from all organisation, that, even with the wisest conduct on the part of Catholics, there is no hope, humanly speaking, of this melancholy and incurable division being healed by the return of the Protestants as a body to the Church. But the best among them are now nearer to the Church than they have ever been before, and desire nothing more ardently than to return into the bosom of Catholic unity. We can hear their heart-rending lamentations, that it is sought to make this impossible to them. For it is precisely the best among them who could not possibly hold Catholicism and curialism to be identical. And what was never thought of in the

16th, 17th, or 18th, and only quite recently in the 19th century, that they should be required to hold curialism, with all its consequences, to be Catholicism, is what is now exacted from them, and we are seeking to render the burden still more intolerable.

With regard also to the Oriental schismatics, and especially the Russians, whose Church is wholly degenerate, even with the wisest conduct on the part of Catholics, there is no hope, humanly speaking, of a return of the bulk of the people to Catholic unity at this time, since petrifaction on the one hand, and on the other dissolution, are visibly going on. But many individuals, and perhaps whole bodies, might still be won back—and, at all events, that precious portion of the Catholic Church, the United Greeks, who have been so unjustifiably neglected, or so harshly dealt with, might be knit together in closer bonds of living union, and intercommunion with them freshly and healthily quickened. But from what is now unmistakably, and, according to the *Civilta* and many other papers, undoubtedly, in preparation, and of which a Catholic paper* said naively not long since, "that now is the time to hold a Council, because there is not always, and indeed scarcely ever has been, an episcopate at hand composed like the present;" it is impossible to hope for any wholesome effect upon the Orientals, either upon the Uniates, however much they may need it, or upon the schismatics.

Oh that we were able, and that all those more worthy and capable than we are, and those whose position in the Church is in any way influential and who do not refuse the responsibility thus imposed upon them, were able, by at least pointing out the unhappy and inevitable consequences

* We unfortunately neglected to make a note of the passage, and we do not even know if it was in the *Theologisches Literaturblatt*—in which articles have occasionally appeared of late in striking contrast to the excellent ones generally found in it—or in the *Augsburger Postzeitung*. We can answer, however, for the sense, and even for the verbal accuracy of this characteristic statement.

of the unheard-of measures now projected, and by entreaties for the love of the Divine Saviour, to cause the abandonment of these most unprecedented designs! Oh ye shepherds appointed to feed the flock in Christ's stead! and thou so sadly torn and scattered flock, attacked by enemies without, and sorely perturbed within! Look around you! Compare the picture the Church once offered, with that which it now presents! Look upon the real promoters, the intellectual authors of the present state of things, upon those who saw their own frustrated aims promoted, and a *tabula rasa* made for their success by the ruins left behind by the revolutions, the sole work of which was destruction and dismemberment, and which could neither construct nor unite. Look upon a Lamennais, a Bonald, a de Maistre, and even a Görres, and a Binterim. Weigh them in the balances of the sanctuary against the sterling teachers of the Church in all ages since the Fathers. The terrible end of the priest Lamennais is well known, but the process of development leading to that end is not so well known as it ought to be for the appreciation of the cause of which he was the coryphaeus. Of the others we will say nothing here, as a searching treatment would be necessary. We only repeat, Examine, weigh, and compare them with the great teachers God has granted to His Church until our own times.

What strength to resist existed formerly in the Church, even in the most difficult circumstances; and what weakness now! What life circulated in all its parts! What a spirit of union formerly manifested itself, and now, except where party spirit prevails, what a spirit of isolation! What clear manifestations and rich fruits of that life were formerly to be seen, and now, how troubled, broken, unsatisfying, and out of all organic coherence, are all its manifestations and fruits! What lavish expenditure upon the shell, while the spirit, the reality, the kernel is left uncared for! What a recognition the Church's life then extorted from the world, and what hatred it now meets with,—when it does not reap for itself scorn or contempt!

A faithful servant of the Church might now serve her by preparing a new edition of Bossuet's *Exposition de la Foi Catholique*, with all the documents by which it is solemnly authorised, and a preface pointing out its agreement with all other truly Catholic expositions of the orthodox faith of the Church. It would be a good *Vade Mecum* for every Bishop present at the council.

The future, for which the Society of Loyola—already modernised for the purpose—with its partizans, thinks to make provision, belongs not to them. It belongs to the Eternal and Unchangeable King, to whom our hearts should be unceasingly lifted up in the prayer at the end of the Holy Scriptures, "Even so, come Lord Jesus, come quickly;" and again, "Send forth Thy Spirit, and all things shall be created, and Thou shalt renew the face of the earth." (1 Tim. i. 17; Rev. xxii. 20; Ps. ciii. 32.)

But we have first a time of trial to expect, of which we are warned by a sacred tradition, in the line of which we find the holy Pope, Gregory the Great, and which is borne witness to by the deep researches of great men enlightened from above. This time of trial appears to be already far advanced. But pessimism is never allowable. We must fight to the last moment, and rally round our flag to our last breath. It has been our desire to fulfil this duty to the utmost of our feeble powers.

O God, the fountain of all truth and righteousness, Thou who canst love nothing but what is perfectly true and perfectly righteous, Thou who crownest in secret those who suffer unto death and unto the loss of all things for the sake of truth and righteousness, as Thou alone, who seest in secret, knowest the measure of their sufferings, grant us grace even in the greatest darkening of

Thy truth, and the greatest disfigurement of the countenance of Thy beloved Church, to abide loyally in her, to love her more heartily as she becomes more like Thy Son in His bitter suffering, and to live and die in the profession and practice of the pure, genuine and inviolate ancient Catholic faith, in the exercise of love, perseverance, and patience.

Grant us this grace through the intercession of our predecessors in this worst of martyrdoms.

We beg this through our Lord Jesus Christ, Thy Son, who, with Thee, O Father, and in the unity of the Holy Ghost, liveth and reigneth, one God, world without end. Amen.

APPENDIX I.

BOSSUET holds a quite exceptional position in the Church. It approaches so nearly to that of one of the Fathers, when considered in relation to the last centuries and their peculiar needs, that we feel compelled to say a few words respecting him, especially as the German clergy, educated within the last twenty years, need some information with respect to this great light of the Church. An introductory remark is first necessary. It belongs to the nature of mathematical science that, in so far as it concerns pure mathematics, it does not suffer from the influence of particular schools. The mathematical whims which appear occasionally necessarily remain individual. In what concerns astronomy, and in general all applied mathematics, physics, and other natural sciences, a false and narrow school has no evil influence on those minds of the first eminence which are able to break its chains, but this is less true in regard to the various provinces of art, because here the temper and will affect the judgment of what is beautiful. Still less, as a rule, is a false, erroneous, and one-sided school without injurious influence even upon a mind of the first class, which withdraws itself from its dominion in its search after philosophical truth. The same may be said of the application of philosophy to practical life, of the administration of justice, and of political and economic science. Least of all, however, as a rule, is this injurious influence absent in theology. The cause of this lies in the nature of this science, whose office it is to unite heaven and earth, time and eternity, and in the manner in which the workings of grace lie hidden in the human mind. Most rarely does it happen that even an instrument of God is able to

APPENDIX I.

free himself so entirely as did St Paul from the false school to which he once belonged, while so instantaneous a conversion as he underwent is not less uncommon in the history of the kingdom of God.

Bossuet's only teachers were men who were thoroughly dominated by the spirit of the Society of Loyola, in the shape that spirit, favoured by what was abnormal in the first foundation of the society, had already taken, and which had attained to a decided mastery in the seventeenth century. From this false teaching the powerful genius and lofty character of Bossuet wholly freed itself, without other support moreover, up to a certain point, than the fundamental character which was the traditional heirloom of that glorious branch of the Universal Church—now languishing in miserable weakness—to which he belonged by birth. It does the great man much honour, that he strove after and attained to so clear a discernment of the truth, and to so profound a theology, though he did not wholly escape the injurious influence of his early training. This betrays itself in certain defects of his theology, which took the form, partly of aberrations (*ecarts*, as the French would say), and partly of a striking one-sidedness in the examination of the Prophetical Books,—defects which, however, only affected his general conduct in particular occurrences and unimportant moments of his priestly career, and which were without the slightest influence upon any of his great and important theological works. Some disavowed occasional pieces of his youth, some few unimportant productions of his genius, consisting chiefly of letters, and his Exposition of the Apocalypse, alone among his writings show tokens of these defects. And with regard to this last work, the great prelate (who governed his diocese so blamelessly, and fed the flock committed to his care with a spiritual zeal equal to his greatness as a theologian) allowed himself to be won over in his later years by Duguet, whom he highly esteemed, to sounder and juster views, and of this change in his opinions many traces are visible in the sterling works of his old age. We had much more to say of the man who, in his lifetime, was the light of Israel, and a living barrier against all excess of evil and error, but we reserve it for another occasion. Significant indeed of the difference between his times and our own is the circumstance—and here we entirely agree with the learned author of the article on "The Council and the *Civiltà*," in the *Allgemeine Zeitung*, of March 1869—that Providence assigned the same office, that of being a living barrier against all excess of evil and error, to Bishop Melchior of Diepenbrock in our own day. What a distance there is between the genius and theological depth of a Bossuet and a Diepenbrock! It is the difference of the times in reference to the Church, which is reflected in the difference which exists between these two Prelates. But in pure and lofty will, in love to the Lord and His Church, in faithfulness as Christians and Priests, and in boldness in the service of truth,

—none have worked so vigorously to disperse the mists which have arisen from the school to which they both once belonged—in all these exalted qualities by which God will judge His servants, these two stand at least very near each other, as great lights of the Church.

For once more we must contradict the miserable calumnies of these modern pigmies, and we are always ready to prove what we assert. Bossuet was indeed a strong monarchist, and he lived at a time when royal absolutism had attained its highest point; but that old royal absolutism, when not spurred on and abused by men like the confessors of Louis XIV., (especially the last of them, the truly detestable Latellier), all belonging to the Jesuits, was much limited by regard to custom, as well as by a hundred ordinances, while the revolutionary absolutism of our days, whether supported by the fiction of a constitution it exerts authority from above, or raves in wild agitation from below, in all circumstances, scattering destruction in its train, acknowledges neither respect nor restraint, neither law nor custom. Yet notwithstanding his politics, Bossuet never spared the king in the smallest degree from hearing the truth, although his dutiful subject in all worldly matters, according to the appointment of Divine Providence. It is not to be conceived what he might have accomplished had he been the King's Diocesan, instead of a Hardouin de Beaumont, a Harlay, or even instead of that honest theologian and pious Priest, but weak Prelate, de Noailles. Louis XIV., who felt towards the great man a fear analagous to the slavish fear of God, from which he could not free himself,— and among those who approached him, he called Bossuet, the one spotless servant of his God,—Louis XIV., who was equally unwilling to forsake sin or to fall into hell, carefully avoided placing Bossuet in the Episcopal See of his chief city. It must, however, be acknowedged, that under the rule of Louis XIV., many worthy bishops became a blessing to the Church of France, and the Catholic

Church in general, although afterwards he oppressed, and even persecuted, several of them. And this fatal right of nomination, which is entirely irreconcileable with the true constitution of the Church, the Roman *Curia*, to whom it does not belong, has granted to kings, who are not fit to receive it, in order to obtain other favours in exchange, a bargain by which, as has been said before, the contracting parties give to each other that which belongs to neither of them.

APPENDIX II.

IT is much to be wished that the Governments of Europe may learn what a future they are helping to prepare when they direct their efforts against Christianity, and consequently (speaking from the point of view of a philosopher and a statesman) against the groundwork of all that is truly noble in our civilisation; and that they may become aware that they are deceived and betrayed by parties who take advantage of their miserable blindness to attempt to usurp their power, and who assist each other in this attempt as long as the work to be done is one of ruin and destruction, and then, when the question is of establishing new things in the place of what has been destroyed, turn their arms against each other. Would that the Governments with truly statesmanlike foresight would learn further, to what it must lead, if the relations of the Church with the State, which are grounded upon and have grown out of the principles of Christianity, are looked upon as foreign to the State, which must soon lead to their mutual relations being regarded and treated as hostile on both sides.

The *jus circa sacra* which belongs to the State is an inalienable right, like that which belongs to our earthly parents, although both are liable to be, and are, wickedly misused. A State which consents to forego this right, disowns what is of the very essence of human nature. It is the duty of the State to exercise this right with strict justice and equity. Even under the Roman Empire, in the earliest centuries of Christianity, when it was not possible to keep clear of the civil law and State assistance, Christians appealed to them under the empire of Pagan Rome, before it had undertaken the task of destroying the Church, and in those intervals of refreshment which they always enjoyed from time to time afterwards, during the unparalleled war which seemingly was waged by a power of the most enormous material superiority, in combination with the whole civilisation, intelligence and art of heathendom, against a body totally powerless both in fact and theory, but which was really waged by the world against Almighty God. How much rather must this appeal be considered legitimate in our States, and in the interests of both the great powers alike, whereof the one exists by the immediate appointment of God and only attains to its consummation in eternity, while the other is not less, though mediately, willed and appointed by God, that it may serve as a school wherein man should ripen for that eternal life, and be prepared through the ordinances of this world, whose fashion passeth away,* for the true and eternal order of the kingdom of heaven. How much rather, we repeat, must it be true of our States,

* 1 Cor. vii. 31.

and be acknowledged to be for the interest of both Church and State, that the *jus circa sacra* is their inalienable right. The very foundations of our States are rooted in the soil of Christianity. The *appellationes de abusu* belong to their very nature. How, for instance, could a Christian Government permit an absolute tyranny to oppress a Bishop and paralyse his right of action, or to suspend a priest, even were he in the lowliest position in the eyes of the world, and eventually to depose him, and perhaps deprive him of the exercise of the indelible and inherent rights belonging to his sacred character and interdict him from the performance of his holy functions, to the great injury of souls and of the whole Church? How, again, could they allow the holy sacraments to be publicly refused to an honest and irreproachable Christian, against whom not the shadow of real transgression of the laws of God or of the ordinances of the Church can be proved, and whose only reproach is that he clings to that which alone can be a law to a true child and servant of the Church more firmly than is agreeable to the supporters of the modern system?

Perfidious enemies of religion, like Julian the Apostate, may indeed intend the destruction of Christianity by such an abdication of their highest powers, and they will attain their accursed end when the hour of Divine punishment is come for their country; but in the midst of what terrible phenomena and with what destructive results for the State! This consideration ought to decide the attitude towards the Council of those governments which are at the head of nations, either entirely or in great part Catholic. Essentially non-Catholic governments could of course only be admitted to the Council in connection with such Governments as are at the head of States which can be looked upon as essentially Catholic.

In this place we can only give these few hints. They are sufficient, where there is a good will, to lead to a search for further information: where that is absent, the most thorough examination would be in vain.

We have still something to say here upon curialism, and upon its latest and most extravagant exaggerations.

This system arose gradually, and ecclesiastical history shows how, and points out the circumstances and events which have made possible, occasioned, and furthered its growth and unmistakeable exaggerations in the course of the middle ages. Political and ecclesiastical history alike tell us what mischief it has done, for the real good which the Primate has effected, was effected not because, but in spite of the influence of this system, which has been as injurious to him as to the Church in general.

In its earlier and more tolerable form this system was only capable of leading into error because, as in all error, a grain of truth lay at its foundation, or rather, let us say, because it owed its origin to a legitimate desire pointing to a future reality for our own age.

This desire proceeds from the continual remembrance of the need of a higher state of perfection. It found its satisfaction in a temporary realisation as long as it was necessary, that is, in the Apostolic age; but it will only find its true and lasting satisfaction in a consummation and perfection prophetically promised to us hereafter. It is the desire for a dispensation of spiritual gifts duly subordinated to episcopal superintendence, which will, strictly speaking, be vouchsafed to the Church, when she attains to the fulness of the stature of Christ,* and, as we are persuaded, before her destiny in this world is accomplished and has reached its final close. It will then be hers through Him who is the true Head of His Church, because He is the First-born

* "Non dormitabit neque dormiet qui custodit Ecclesiam; is nimirum qui ascendens in altum dedit quosdam quidem Apostolos, quosdam autem Prophetas, alios vero Evangelistas, alios Pastores et Doctores, ad consummationem Sanctorum, in opus ministerii, in ædificationem corporis Christi, donec occurramus omnes in unitatem fidei et agnitionis Filii Dei, in virum perfectum, in mensuram ætatis plenitudinis Christi" (*Concil. Senon.* ann. 1528, Dec. 1.) This decree is drawn up in exact accordance with Scripture, and we see here again that the Church was able to repel heresy and schism only by a declaration of the perfect truth, never by an ap-

of all creatures, the true Bishop and Shepherd of our souls, the real Apostle of God (Heb. iii. 1) and the faithful Witness (Ap. 15); for the early Christians—*e.g.* the truly glorious martyrs of Lyons—often said that to Him alone belonged the name of Martyr. The Church rejoiced in this administration through the spiritual gifts in her temporary and imperfect state of consummation, during the time the Apostles of our Lord carried on its government in this world, and while the last survivor of them, St John, carried it on alone, and was in so far at its head, whether he dwelt in Rome or in exile at Patmos or in Ephesus. This was a necessary dispensation of Providence for the safety of the Catholic Church,

plication of the curialistic system. We know that the grounds of what has been said above, about a fulfilment of the desire spoken of being to be looked for before the end of the world, requires to be more fully stated and explained. But although we are at all times ready, this is not the place for it. Only we thought we ought to intimate so much, in view of the excessively gloomy prospect the immediate future offers to us. For, if we must now sigh at every moment, saying, "Where is Israel's light and strength, where is Israel's glory?" it will the more be our duty to wait for the consolation of Israel.

until she had gained strength to support herself against the synagogue, which had broken off from her, and the heathen world—against, that is, an abused authority which had turned against its Giver—and to preserve herself in a state of purity, free from any admixture of heresy, against a wholly illegitimate and monstrous authority; until she was strong enough to enter upon and maintain the difficult struggle incumbent on her for so many centuries, as the limiting and guiding principle in the centre of the most important developments of human nature. In the same way that the long lives of the Patriarchs before the flood, and of the later Patriarchs, although considerably shortened, for fifteen hundred years after, must have been the greatest blessing, the first to the whole of mankind, and the last to true religion, as Pascal has so justly remarked and so beautifully explained (*Pensées*, Tit. xii. of the original edition), so the prolonged life of the Apostle John, the most spotless and best beloved among the

Twelve, has been the greatest blessing to the Church of the New Covenant.

It is just this remarkable ἀντίτυπον (antitype) and πρόπλασμα of the New Testament, in the earlier history of the Church, which is the model and pattern alike of the fulfilment of that whereof curialism sets before our eyes a distorted and false counterfeit, a veritable ἀνομοιότης (a representation which is unlike and of a wholly different nature). This antitype embarrasses the curialists, particularly their modern leaders, who run into the greatest extravagances, and would gladly throw the holy Apostle and Prophet of the Apocalypse into the shade, and who even presume to maintain that he entirely abandoned the chief government of the Church to Cletus and Clemens of Rome, and that this subordinate position was his fitting place. Is it possible to look upon Christian antiquity, and especially the Apostolic age, through a more deceptive medium? On the other hand, we find most satisfactory evidence of the exact contrary of this arbitrary assertion in the New Testament narrative of the questions addressed by the disciples to their risen Lord on the Sea of Tiberias, and of their misunderstanding His answer, and also in many circumstances in the life of the Church and passages in its liturgy; in the text of the Preface on the feasts of Apostles, according to the Roman missal, for example.

Curialism in its present extravagance is filling up the measure of its errors by becoming guilty of the same abuse of the legitimate idea of development, in its application to the history of the Church, as Hegel and his followers in respect to its application to the history of mankind. Instead of the guidance of a regular and healthy organic action of the Church by the Holy Ghost, this system sets up a pretended inspiration like that to which the Quakers lay claim, and in reality it is the Pope alone to whom this inspiration is supposed to belong, as the genuineness of the inspiration bestowed upon the other Bishops must be tested by the inspiration bestowed upon him.

In its latest invention of so-called latent dogmas, in which it does not allow itself to be in the least disturbed by the providentially ordered exact determination of the date of the origin and first appearance of an opinion, or by the most solemn and uninterrupted opposition to it from the time of its first becoming known, curialism places itself upon a level with the fiction of a so-called invisible Church, which was necessary to the earlier Protestants in order to enable them to hold fast positive Christianity without a real Church. With its unlimited law of development, as it now presents it, it stands upon precisely the same ground as Hegelianism: for, according to it, all is legitimate, all is healthy development, which has arisen and actually exists in the Church with the express or silent approbation of Rome; and as Schleiermacher says that the Holy Ghost can be nothing but the—according to him, constantly mutable—spirit of the Christian community, curialism, in its present extreme, desires to see temporary ideas, prevalent during a small portion of the lifetime of Christianity, and which after being current for some time as opinions have been formulized by the Pope speaking *ex cathedrâ*, and accepted by a completely dependant episcopate, declared to be decrees of the Church —of the Church, which to-day is the same body it was in the days of the Apostles, and throughout all Christian antiquity, and which cannot disclose anything to be believed explicitly now which was only believed, as is pretended, implicitly of old. The only difference to be found between curialism and the teaching of Schleiermacher, is that the former, as it cannot wholly deny its external connection with the true Catholic doctrine, is obliged to admit and keep in view a final consummation of all things in eternity, while Schleiermacher appears to hold this to be an impossibility. But how does such an innovation agree with the warning of the Holy Ghost? " Remove not the ancient landmarks, which thy fathers have set." (Proverbs xxii. 28.) It is forgotten that Christian antiquity is to be our pattern and example throughout all time, so that every deviation from its mind and character is no healthy development, but a sickly affection, if not altogether an aberration; and that in piety, as in all else, Christian antiquity must be our example in every respect, as to the right measure and degree of what we are to strive after. Where is any attention still paid to the Apostolic warning in the Epistle to the Romans? (xii. 3.) Where is the $\phi\rho\text{ονεῖν}$ εἰς τὸ $\sigma\omega\phi\rho\text{ονεῖν}$, the circumspect, rightly judging, truly prudent temperance, modesty and chastity, which we are admonished to exercise in all things, in thought and in inclination, the *sapere ad sobrietatem* of the Vulgate?

The acknowledgment of the Divine protection which is promised to the Church, does not in any way distinguish Curialism from the school of Hegel. Hegel also claims a Divine protection for his development, and thus justifies his unconditional recognition of all that has come into being and exists. It is not worth while to inquire what the poor philosopher figures to himself under the sacred name of God, the main question being, whether the conditions are fulfilled under which alone the Divine protection, the guidance of the Holy Spirit shielding us from all error, can take effect.

And in what large characters and with what striking colours sacred and profane history alike contradict this arbitrary assumption. How can Divine harmony and beauty be more unjustifiably disfigured? How can it be forgotten what fatal influence sin, and the weakness which proceeds from sin, and the error which is its result, are able to gain and often to maintain for a long time over this—doubtless divinely appointed and therefore necessary and undeniable—development; and all the more, the longer the duration of this sickly deformity, which is at once an excess and in some sense an atrophy!

Who can believe the strange abortions of the middle ages to have been a thoroughly healthy development? It is because they were not so, that they contributed so powerfully to the unhappy schism of the Greeks and the Orientals under their influence, which was not on that account, however, less unjustifiable, both materially and formally. It is true that in the middle ages these developments were formed, received and held fast in simple faith, by upright and often touchingly sincere Christian minds and intellects, to whom nothing was wanting but the thorough Christian culture of sacred antiquity, and that, under God's providence, they produced abundant good effects in individuals. Now, on the contrary, in their modern completely degenerate and abnormal form, they are no longer clung to in simple faith, but held sophistically; not excused as a lesser and temporary evil to be borne with, but defended as in harmony with the original idea. They are naturally, therefore, laughed to scorn by a world which has quite outgrown the circumstances which gave them birth, and which becomes daily more envenomed in its hatred, more immoderate in its calumnies against Christ and His Church, and more reckless in the choice of the vilest means to—as it imagines—annihilate Christ and His kingdom. Who can accept these strange and sometimes monstrous abortions as a thoroughly healthy development? Certainly not those who have been nourished with the solid food of Christian antiquity.

The excellent Adrian VI., whose pontificate is a most striking proof of God's care for His Church, was certainly a thoroughly scholar-like statesman, as he proved in Spain, when his former pupil, Charles V., then still young, was willing to bestow his confidence upon him in the affairs of government. The great Ximenes de Cisneros, great as a statesman and as a scholar and enlightened promoter of civilisation, who stands before us in such incomparable purity by the side of the thoroughly modern Richelieu — the remarkable prelate and statesman who came from the family of St Francis—was equal to encounter the difficulties of civil government, and was not far distant in ability from Adrian the son of the citizen of

Utrecht. But he received his theological education under the influence of those ideas (then indeed still received in simplicity) which must be described as abnormal in an ecclesiastical point of view, and which modern civilisation, so essentially Christian, and on that account alone so indestructible and so powerful, had not then entirely outgrown. He was surpassed as a theologian by Adrian, who was in that respect better fitted for the government and guidance of the Church. Now let us look at this excellent chief pastor in Rome, and compare him with his successors, who either were not theologians at all (as it must be honestly confessed, was usually the case in the seventeenth century), or in whom, as with the popes from Clement VII. to Paul V. inclusively, the theologian was completely absorbed in the statesman, so that only Clement IX., Innocent XI., Innocent XII., Benedict XIII., Benedict XIV., and Clement XIV., can be characterised more or less as true theologians and in the first rank as Bishops and Popes in a purely ecclesiastical sense.* The character of Adrian VI., thus considered and compared with others, assists us very much in finding the key to decipher and estimate justly what we have called abnormal formations, and which cannot be looked upon as a healthy development in true correspondence with the Divine appointment, and cannot therefore be defended as normal and held unconditionally.

But this brings us to a wide field for discussion, into which we will not enter here. It belongs to those subjects which at the present time are still rightly described as indifferent.

It is not the same with the opinion of the so-called infallibility of the Pope, which cannot be even temporarily reconciled with truth. It is not merely a defective opinion which has grown up, under Divine Providence, for the prevention of

* Benedict XIV., however, showed the one-sidedness of his school, which may also be detected in Pius V.; and hence the examples of both of them may be easily and fatally abused.

greater evils, and is therefore to be allowed—which, if not to be inflexibly maintained, is yet not lightly to be rejected, remembering the French proverb, "que le mieux est (souvent) le plus grand ennemi du bon." We have not in this case to deal with a system which can by any possibility be reconciled with truth and made good use of. No, that theological opinion is a morbid excrescence, towards which all forbearance would be dangerous, and any attempt to smuggle it into the sacred domain of doctrine, under a higher and the only binding title, would be a deadly attack upon the Divine idea and institution of the Church and upon its sacred constitution.

Still the curialistic system, even after it had gradually grown to completeness during the middle ages, was not so dangerous, in a theological sense, at the end of the fifteenth century as it afterwards became. It still shrank with a holy awe from the sacred domain of dogma, and refrained from laying a sacrilegious hand upon the *depositum fidei*, the precious deposit of the faith. The prevalent ignorance had indeed done serious mischief, but the greatest reverence was still felt towards the treasure confided to the Church by God, although, through the almost exclusive influence of scholastic teaching, it was but little known and in many points not accepted in perfect purity. The unrestrained secularisation of the Church, with a colouring from the Old Testament,* was followed by the revival of heathenism in the fourteenth and fifteenth centuries. But even this, fearfully as it injured the religious purity of ecclesiastical life, was not nearly so antipathetic to the precious deposit of the faith as the most modern extreme of curialism. We have already become acquainted with Cardinal a Turrecremata in this period of curialism. Those Popes and leaders of the Roman Court, who held with the Sadducees, troubled themselves little about spiritual and theological

* It was a retrospective anticipation, a πρόληψις παλινόρμενος, *i.e.*, a really and vehemently reactionary conception of the future, in consequence of an obscured and defective representation of the consummation really promised.

matters, and as a rule allowed those who were not given up to worldliness and unbelief to do as they pleased in regard to these matters—"*in mere spiritualibus*," as was said with a good-humoured smile by so many worldly German prelates before the last secularisation. Curialism became more dangerous with Cajetan, in whose works we first meet with the Infallibility of the Pope as a completely formulised theological opinion; and while a true and genuine reforming movement was beginning within the Catholic Church, and was striving to heal and efface the immense injuries of the preceding centuries which had made Protestantism possible, curialism was also establishing itself in its present *theological* form. In the reforming decrees of the Council of Trent the Roman Court was able to secure a loop-hole for itself, and it succeeded, after the close of the Council, in gaining possession of a centralising power stifling all free life. In this it was greatly assisted, beyond its own immediate jurisdiction, by the Spanish Inquisition, the Nunciatures, and above all by the Jesuits, who alone were able to reserve to themselves the privilege of not obeying the *Curia* itself, when its regulations and instructions were not to their taste. It was then that the Gallican Church, *i.e.*, the Church of France, in its genuine form, gained such an immense importance, full of blessings to the whole holy Catholic Church, because she alone among all its great divisions—the national Churches—remained steadfast as a body to the ancient constitution of the Church, as far as that was allowed by the circumstances of the times and the ruinous Concordat concluded between Francis I. and Leo X. Her strength was indeed broken under Louis XV., and especially during the long ministry of Cardinal Fleury, now nearly a hundred and fifty years ago, and that too in the interests of curialism and by the most scandalous means. But her constitution was still untouched, so that she was in a position to begin to recover herself during the latter half of the last century. Scarcely, however, had the fruits of the new life stirring within her and of her faithfully guarded tradition become perceptible, when the great political revolution, which has since spread over Europe and America and in which we still find ourselves involved, burst forth from a soil laid waste by civil and spiritual misrule and broken up by an unbelief, which, thanks to the victory of curialism and so-called Jesuitism, was everywhere predominant.

As we find in every given case the closest mutual relation between the sins of the people and some vice of their Government, we likewise find the same mutual relation between the faults of believers and the state of the clergy and misgovernment, in some way, of the Church; and this is particularly remarkable in our days as regards the Church. The present circumstances of the Church, so thoroughly abnormal and deplorable beyond example, which are now become intolerable, and which it is intended to fix in this condition, were introduced and made possible by an erroneous and false current of opinion emanating from the laity, who, in consequence of the wasting of the vineyard under the influence of curialism and of the society of Loyola, were left without any true Catholic instruction and grasped an illusion instead of the truth, when the ruins of the revolution and the idea-less, atomical, mechanical, life-destroying, life-denying secular *régime* which proceeded from it, had awakened in them a longing for something more worthy of human nature. The great talents, and even the, in a measure, undeniable geniality of these men have unfortunately only served to make the errors to which they were devoted more seducing and more dangerous. Some of them were German Protestants, who did not even profess to belong to the Catholic Church; others were German converts, whose conversion was not of the same genuine nature as that of Count Stolberg, who owed this superiority to what remained of the *ancient* French Church, which exercised the most decided influence upon his conversion; while some were Catholics by birth, but men who, as we have already said, were wholly deficient in sound religious instruction and education in Church principles, and remained to the last dilettantes in theology. We find only one priest, the unhappy Lamennais, among the first leaders of this movement in France. All the others were laymen, and it was the same in Germany. And thus it is from revolutionised France and from Germany, which had been drawn into sympathy with her, that this miserable revolution in the Church has proceeded, having been brought about by the laity, while all previous revolutions in the Church have been brought about by ecclesiastics, as it is natural that the greatest blessings and the greatest misfortunes to the Church should alike proceed from the clergy.

This exceptional origin of a revolution which, within the limits of the Catholic community, has essentially altered the constitution of the Catholic Church, and disfigured her to such an extent that she cannot be recognised, ought to be closely observed. Through it curialism has reached its latest, most unmeasured extreme, and gained its deadening, absolute sway. This terrible consequence would indeed have been impossible, if the political revolution had not previously ruined and destroyed every thing, nor was it completely realised until after the disappearance of the last correct recollection of the ancient ecclesiastical and genuinely Catholic conditions and regulations, principles and practices, owing to the continually progressive estrangement and separation of the mass of the people from Christian principles, which took place under the influence of this disfigurement, the faults of neglect even more than of commission occasioned thereby on the part of the Governments, and the consequent continual fresh outbreaks and progress of the revolution.

The modern Pseudo-traditionalists have in later days opposed the modern Loyolistic scholiasts, especially in France. They sometimes rectify their errors, sometimes not, or they only put one error, that is generally a distorted original truth, in the place of another distortion of truth, *i.e.*, another error; never, however, with equal genius, and with only approximate cleverness. Their organisation, however, gained them the victory; the two tendencies have since then been amalgamated, and thus the state of the Church most acceptable to curialism has grown up, and, if their plans succeed, is to be established in perpetuity. They imagine at least that they can make it permanent.

What have been the consequences of this to our Lord's dearly purchased inheritance, the Church? The life of the community is completely destroyed, its history denied, its ancient customs done away with; the instruction given is no longer merely insufficient, but directly confusing, and by its terrible dryness prepares men's minds and souls for apostasy and death. The subsequent teaching by sermons is either of the same nature as the catechetical or, if it is better, there is no preparation or capacity in the minds of the hearers to derive benefit from it. It is a foreign language, which at the utmost can only excite wonder, but to which generally no attention is paid because it is not understood. Nothing is put into practice and nothing is read, or mere outward exercises and alien devotions in a foreign tongue take the place of those efficacious practices, prayer and spiritual reading, which nourish the soul and promote progress in the inner life. Nowhere do we hear of the Holy Scriptures, nowhere of an even moderate knowledge and appreciation of the life of the Church, of any participation in the inexhaustible treasury of her liturgical hymns and prayers, or of the excellent books of former centuries. Paltry or at best indifferent books, which are daily fabricated in immense numbers and obtain publicity, are offered to those who still feel some hunger after knowledge, and who have not already, from want of nourishment, lost the feeling of its necessity and almost the capacity for receiving it. This is true with respect to the faithful of every age, sex and condition, and of every degree of mental cultivation. For something better or even more or less good appears from time to time for the use of theologians—at least in Germany, very little in France, and one may say nothing in Spain, Italy and other countries—and even something excellent in the sciences auxiliary to theology, which brings to light real acquisitions to knowledge; yet among these books also the greater number are indifferent, or even bad, while what is good seldom meets with minds prepared for its right and full use, and hence remains isolated and without efficacy to promote spiritual life. As to Church discipline for the people, the shadow of such a thing is not remotely mentioned. The very memory of it has disappeared. The most wholesome admonitions and regulations of the Church, being entirely unintelligible and considered as an arbitrary imposition, are only observed formally and in the letter, without love or devotion, nay often in defiance of their spirit and intention, or else are wholly neglected. Much more might be said in explanation of these subjects in detail, and most numerous, various and melancholy examples of what is here asserted could be produced.

There must on no account be any national ritual, however ancient, beautiful and venerable; all must be according to the modern Roman use, and every clergyman must slavishly submit to this hitherto unexampled tyranny. Examples of this mode of treatment are numerous, most numerous and most unmeasured in the France of the present day and in Italy. Any observance of ecclesiastical law is out of the question. Even the privilege of being irremovable, where it still exists, is scarcely a protection, especially as the State is unconscious of its duty respecting it, and of its great interest in the safety of religion, and the Governments take up rather the attitude of enemies than protectors to the Church. But even this slight restraint is apparently to be set aside, and the truly revolutionary abolition of the irremovability of the clergy is an ideal striven after.* And if in any ecclesiastical history, or other theological work, any truth or fact unpleasing to the curialists is discussed, the book is forbidden, and its author cried down; and if he belong to the clergy, unless he submits, as it is called, blindly, contrary to the laws of Christian morality no less than of merely social honour, the course of vexatious annoyances mentioned above is begun against him, without his being allowed a hearing, or even a knowledge of what error he is accused of, and why? †

On the other hand, it may happen, as the newspapers of the province of Drenthe informed us last year, that a priest who, on all grounds of law and good morals, ought never again to have approached the altar, is re-admitted to his sacred functions.

* [The parish priests in France have lost their canonical rights by the Concordat, and are removable at the arbitrary will of the Bishop, like a curate in the Church of England.—Tr.]

† It is evident that the idea of humility is no less thoroughly perverted than the ideas of faith and of Christian obedience, since such behaviour is called in official language, "a laudable submission." See pp. 55-57 and 68-69 note, as well as note, pp. 76-77.

There are parishes almost always entrusted to such persons, more or less distinctly disqualified, and the people may, *e.g.*, take part in matters wholly incompatible with their Christian profession, and read papers daily filled with the most odious blasphemies, while the young are allowed to grow up under these influences and impressions, without the slightest attempt being made to enforce the discipline of the Church.

The so-called Catholic daily press consists, however, of two classes of papers: one is edited by men who, however deserving of respect they may be—and some of them, to our own knowledge, really are so—are yet unlearned zealots in religion, and exercise in this respect a most injurious influence upon their readers: the papers of the other class groan under a party tyranny which compels them to exclude from their pages every convincingly true, every convincingly powerful word. And thus a well-instructed Catholic, who is truly devoted to his Church, can nowhere find a possibility of giving utterance to the pure truth, unless he resolves to beg for it from strangers to his Church, as nothing could induce him to ask it of open enemies and blasphemers. Only such sins of omission and commission render it explicable that, for instance, in the late elections, preponderating Catholic populations, like those of Munich, Würzburg and other places, were persuaded—in Munich almost to a man, and by great majorities in the others—either to abstain from voting altogether, or to vote with the destructive party of the revolution, with the worst enemies of their Church and country. And even newspapers of respectable standing, such as the Augsburg *Postzeitung*, occasionally have articles forced upon them which are beneath all criticism, in which very poor writers seek to attack the most able theologians, and in doing so betray an ignorance and incapacity which surpass all description.

Even scientific journals no longer venture to

refuse space to the greatest impertinences, or, what would be still better, to furnish a complete refutation of them by way of corrective. In short, manly and priestly courage are but rarely found under the present system of government, because it needs heroic courage to show either one or the other.

If we agree with the historico-political newspapers upon any subject, when it is brought under our notice, it is, generally speaking, on questions and affairs of public economy, having ourselves studied for some years past these problems now become so fearfully perilous. But what a turn did we lately find given to the conclusion of an article published by the Augsburg *Postzeitung* in its supplement. "The Government of the present ruler of France makes no effort to cure these terrible evils (so excessively aggravated by this neglect), it allows all authority to be set at nought, without hindrance or punishment, and has no other care than to render the assembling of the Council useless, or at least, to prevent its undertaking any thing contrary to the so-called liberties of the Gallican Church," which with the partly real, partly assumed, ignorance common in our days, are described as an invention of Louis XIV. and a fabrication of the year 1682, and the conductor of the paper adds a remark to the effect, "that the Bavarian Government apparently cherishes the same ideas."

What dotage at the end of an article, which, in other respects, contains much that is true and deserving of consideration!

We will not waste words in this place upon the present ruler of France and his conduct. We merely will and must remark, that no one can surpass us in the feeling of aversion which that conduct inspires in every respect, and the conviction that its profligacy has never been equalled in any place during the Christian era, both in what has been done and what has been left undone, in France itself, in Italy, in the East (when it has not been necessary to follow the ancient French traditions), in Germany and in short everywhere.

That the son of Hortensia feels no interest in the Catholic Church for its own sake, cannot admit of a doubt in the mind of an unprejudiced observer. It would so far be a matter of perfect indifference to him, if the most extraordinary attacks were undertaken in the name of the Church herself upon her divinely appointed constitution and her deposit of faith, tradition and history, which must appear to him and his confidants the surest symptoms of its approaching destruction. They calculate that, "any institution which is unfaithful to its principle of life, its origin and essential nature, is near its downfall." In these enterprises, hitherto unheard of and declared impossible, of which we have been and still are to be witnesses, and wherein a faint-hearted love corresponding to a faint-hearted faith sees nothing abnormal, while an ignorant and ill-advised fanaticism hails in them the triumph of the

Church; in all this his eye, sharpened by hatred and antipathy (for hatred sees more keenly than love, when love does not rise to the height of its object and of its mission), discerns the approach of the ignominious ruin which he and his party hold to be possible. Personally, therefore, the present ruler of France would find nothing to object to in the most extravagant plans of the curialists. If his phlegmatic constitution did not allow him to feel any lively joy, he would yet look on with a certain satisfaction at the process of dissolution, which all must expect who are witnesses of these things, and who are without faith in the divine foundation of the Church and in the promises made to her. If anything determines him not to remain entirely passive and gaze upon the realisation of all the dreams of the curialists with a malicious joy, it is only the apprehension he must feel as a statesman of what would probably follow, if the people should lose the remnant of religion which still survives in the country, and, in a measure, even in towns. Probably he only wishes to protract the process of dissolution, in order to gain time for the thorough inoculation of the people with the new religion of Freemasonry, which is so much facilitated by the deplorable state of things in the Church, and which, according to the dream of these men, is to be substituted for Christianity and to make civil society and the enjoyment of life possible—the enjoyment of the present moment of which they lament, with the poet, that men call to it in vain:

"Abide awhile, so fair art thou."

He sees too clearly that the realisation of the extraordinary plans of the curialists will deal a heavy blow to religion, or rather—since religion and its necessary and divinely appointed organ, the Church, cannot perish—that it will lead to those nations, which are still more or less Christian, losing the last remains of Christianity, to their great misery in time and in eternity.

This knowledge—and it is shameful for men, who ught above all others to understand the nature of our holy religion, to be ignorant of it—can be the only reason to induce a man like the present ruler of France to wish to put a check upon the realisation of those extravagant plans, if general report is to be relied upon. The unchristianising of the nations comes too soon; in his opinion they are not yet ripe for it. His idea is, that the new form must be found before the old one is entirely broken to pieces.

God's thoughts are other thoughts; they are high above all the thoughts of the poor children of men. If it shall please Him to grant a happy issue to an opposition, which must be beneficial in itself, from whatever motives it may proceed, we will return Him hearty thanks that He still spares our weakness, remembering the words of our Lord, "Pray ye that your flight be not in the winter, neither upon the Sabbath-day";* that is, that it may not be necessary while you are still more or less ensnared by the love of this world, or still

* Matt. xxiv. 20.

need the indulgence which can seldom be dispensed with by beginners, in the first days of their conversion to a truly Christian life; and we will not regard what instruments His Providence has made use of for this end. Evil and deplorable enough it will be, if these instruments cannot be found in the apostolic judgment, constancy and faithfulness of the greater number of the Bishops, and if therefore God's Providence has to make use, for the protection of His people, of the Governments which are now at the head of the remaining Catholic countries, France, Spain, Austria, Portugal (Italy, alas! is no longer to be reckoned among them*), Belgium, Bavaria, and personally perhaps the excellent King of Saxony,—States which in

---

* The reason of this is that the mongrel product of the revolution, which exists there, has neither history nor solid foundation It is a thing of yesterday, a work of revolutionary caprice and dead abstraction equally incapable of living or dying. Switzerland, too, the half of which is properly one of the Catholic powers, is in so deplorable a condition, that she must be looked upon as lost. The world has provided for the disappearance of the other Catholic Governments and States.

better times earned their greatness, their renown and, so far as they were true to this duty, their prosperity, by their support of the Catholic cause, one may say its preservation for the Christian people of the present day.

This very characteristic of being an essentially Catholic power, in the sense in which we have used the word, has exercised an unavoidable influence upon every French Government, with the exception of the National Convention of 1783, which decreed the denial of the living God.

For the much abused Articles of 1682 are nothing more than the—intentionally weakened—expression of the principles of the ancient and true constitution of the Church, formulised in opposition to the pretensions of the Roman *Curia*. St Louis supported the self-same constitution, and it is to the maintenance of it that the Church of France owed her comparative excellence both in teaching and life, until the unfortunate Concordat, negotiated by Buonaparte and confirmed at the Restoration; the operation of which, however, in its full extent, has only been felt since 1830, and still more strongly since 1848, that is, since the successive revolutions have swept away every obstacle to the tyranny of curialism. And it is to this glory and excellence of the Church of France, with which the ancient university of Paris was so closely connected, that the nation owes her cultivation, her stability, and her strength. This inevitable influence must also be taken into consideration in all the measures adopted by any French Government to prevent any depravation of the essential constitution of the Church in a curialistic sense. It is plain that such a depravation in a Cesaro-papal spirit can never be real or durable in France. And this also is owing to the circumstance, that the French Church has preserved most faithfully the ancient principles of the true constitution of the Church. Should it, however, be too late, and the work begun 300 years ago, and which has made so much progress during the last 150 years, of a complete demolition of the true constitution of the Catholic Church among the nations which are still its support, be already so far advanced that it is no longer possible to put a stop to the fabrication of dogmas, and should the transgression of their first duty in this respect by the Episcopate become as general and as colossal as it seems but too likely to be, in consequence of the unexampled indifference of the faithful with regard to the affairs of the Church and the conduct of the Bishops who are its highest organs, that is, with regard to the body of which they are members—then the hour is come for a judgment, like that which overtook the people of the Old Covenant, when they allowed themselves to be misled by their lawful rulers to reject the Saviour, whom it was their especial mission to announce and wait for, and consequently to acknowledge and worship, to confess and to preach. "Then shall the kingdom of God be taken from this people, and given to a nation bringing forth the fruits thereof."* This leads us

* Matt. xxi. 43.

to another series of considerations, which we must abstain from entering upon in this place.

The audacity with which the declared apostates are already preparing to profit by the impending realisation of the declared plans of the curialists, is shown by the announcement of opposition meetings at Worms and Naples. We describe the meeting to be held at Worms thus, because the complete denial of positive Christianity is expected to be approved there by a large majority.* But these are only isolated and by no means the most suspicious symptoms.

There is still one thing we must dwell upon in answer to the historico-political newspapers. Why is authority now more despised than it ever has been before during the Christian era? Because, during the last centuries, it has been misused within the Catholic Church, as it never was before, to further positive injustice, and to wage a most hateful war upon the most glorious signs

* This has been only too completely realised since.

of life and the most unmistakeable operations of the Holy Ghost; because one authority has constantly striven to injure another; because the true and legitimate authority of the Church has been despised and violated by the Court which surrounds and tyrannises over the first See in Christendom, and the idea of the Church, and of her authority, has been so entirely disfigured as to be no longer recognised by the masses. It was after this had been carried to so great an extent, 150 years ago, with the aid of the secular power, above all in France, where the success of the system was most mischievous, most striking, and most continuous, just because ecclesiastical affairs had remained there up to that time in a comparatively sound condition, that unbelief was able to spread itself so destructively, first in France, and then everywhere else.

Consequently, what the historico-political newspapers, with their mistaken notions of theological and historical truth, propose as a remedy,—and what they blame the present French Government for not adopting, among the many errors to which it pays homage,—is precisely the original cause of the hopeless situation of the nations still considered to be Catholic. And the mere possibility of that state of things, in spite of the activity of pious persons in good works of various kinds, proves the extremely diseased condition of the life of the Church, which we, in common with those newspapers, deplore most deeply and with a sorrow which will only cease with our life.

There is no room for any controversy, properly so called, with the present champions of curialism, of whom the older curialists would be ashamed. One can but drive them away, sword in hand, when their raid upon the—to them inaccessible—domain of sound thought in general, and of theological discipline in particular, seems to render it necessary in any particular case to undertake so distasteful a task. It is the same with them as with the wrong-headed assailants of the Copernican system and the law of gravitation. One can but say to the ignorant, whom they may indeed deceive, "Study it, and you will then know the true upshot of these disputes."*

The case is, in fact, the same in regard to the genuine Catholic doctrine of the Church which belongs to the *depositum fidei*, the unspeakably precious deposit entrusted to her by the Lord, which is the substance of that supernatural revelation, without which the spirit of man left to its own resources could never have attained to the knowledge of Divine truth.

To make the smallest change in this most sacred deposit, under the pretext of intellectual development in its appreciation and thorough comprehension, is the greatest and most dangerous crime.

The Church indeed is never guilty of this. But how little too often does the severe modesty and faithfulness of her Divinely-appointed rulers and

* This is at least most decidedly the case with those adhering to the newest and most monstrous phases of this system, of whom the earliest, perhaps, was Orsi.

her other children correspond with the sacred duties they owe to it, and with the mind of their ever spotless Mother? Yes, she is ever spotless, and her Divinely-kindled life is imperishable. If heavy sickness has so laid hold upon her, that she—whom a penitent well known to us used to call, "the immortal sufferer"*—feels death seizing on her limbs, so that it is only in the heart and in the head that life manifests itself, by imperfect external signs and by feeble, irresolute, seemingly aimless movements; and if she, therefore, cries with the Psalmist, *Ne projicias me in tempore senectutis: cum defecerit virtus mea ne derelinquas me*, yet she thinks of a future which still awaits her in her militant state, in this life, and is revealed in the same Psalm: *Et usque in senectam et senium, Deus, ne derelinquas me, donec annuntiem brachium Tuum generationi omni quae ventura est.*† To this future

* "Malade immortelle" was the name he gave her in the language in which he most frequently conversed with his family and friends.

† Ps. lxx. (Heb. lxxi.) 9, 18.

alone, when rightly conceived and understood, are applicable the beautiful words of Möhler, where he says, "Catholics and Protestants will one day meet in great multitudes, and clasping each other's hands cry out, in a common consciousness of guilt, 'We all have erred, it is the Church alone which cannot err; we all have sinned, she alone is spotless upon earth.'"*

As to the Ratisbon πέτρα *Romana* of Rudis, we must say, in conclusion, that it is a terrible thing, and not to be justified before the Lord, that such indigestible stones should be offered instead of bread to poor Christians, who have to work out their salvation amidst the most grievous difficulties of the present time. Those who are willing to incur this guilt, must truly be wanting in the spirit of Christianity to an incomprehensible degree.

* [*Symbolism*, Eng. Tr., vol. ii. p. 31. These words of "the profound and pious Möhler" are quoted and endorsed with high commendation by Cardinal Wiseman in his famous Letter to Lord Shrewsbury of 1841, p. 33.—Tr.]

SUPPLEMENT

TO THE SECOND EDITION

SINCE the first appearance of these hastily written reflections, many letters to the Author have proved that the favour has been granted to him of being able thereby to help many tortured Catholic souls, and grief-laden Catholic hearts. Amidst the terribly perplexed and truly comfortless circumstances of the times we thank the Lord for this, and pray Him to grant that this and every other word, inspired by the same genuinely Christian and Catholic intention, may yet reach very many Catholics, in order that, where it is needed, more correct ideas of the nature and essence of the Church, our Mother, and of the duties and privileges of the Bishops may be again spread abroad and received into the Catholic conscience; and that where, according to what we see, offence will be taken, either justly or even without sufficient cause, attention may be directed to the right line of conduct to be observed by individuals. May what has been said reach the hearts of very many of our fellow-Christians, who are men of good will!

This wish is the more lively, as we see with deep regret the obstinate blindness, nay, the partly Pharisaic obduracy, with which these fears are represented to the poor believing people as trifling and unnecessary, or suspicion is thrown upon them of being uncatholic and blasphemous. Even the pulpit, which should be set apart for teaching the pure Divine truth, is occasionally misused for this purpose. But, above all, the so-called Catholic daily press puts out on this point what is past all belief. The unfortunate political confusion of our days is of great use in this to curialism, whose diplomacy knows how to secure itself on all sides, to take the hue of all party colours, and to make use of all political parties. To it all is right, Polish or Russian, the party of German unity or the opposite party, legitimacy or the so-called sovereignty of the people, provided only it attains its own ends. And the poor infatuated people, who with their upright hearts take a side which may at least be that of honesty and popular feeling, are deluded in respect to religion by those in whom they recognise, or think they recognise, true sharers of their political opinions. Woe to us that it is so. Would that our political party struggles—which truly are serious enough, and of deep moral importance enough in themselves, as in the last instance they concern the existence of the nations and the stability of civil society—could be fought out, without dragging exclusively religious and ecclesiastical, that is truly theological, questions into the dust of this arena.

There has really no occasion been given for it, except such as has been dragged in, as it were, head and shoulders. For as surely as every political party is deceived which reckons upon the trustworthiness of curialism, so surely there is nothing to be feared from civil Governments at the present time, but their too great indifference to that which ought to be a subject of the most pious solicitude to a Christian and especially a Catholic Government. At most, there is the appearance, in the government of one or other of the small states, of endeavouring to obtain the destruction of positive Christianity. What certain parties, from whom Governments often foolishly dream of finding support, do indeed endeavour to obtain, namely, this very destruction of the Catholic Church and thus of positive Christianity, can never be intended by any Government which is still Catholic. In this matter they remain merely on the defensive, but, alas, without any deep interest in religion and the Church, because without even a moderate knowledge of their true nature. They see themselves threatened by curialism—and here we have not at all in view their other faults, misconceptions, difficulties, and embarrassments—and interfere awkwardly, scarcely ever hitting the right point. And if, for once, they take a right step, it is derided in the most foolish and trifling manner, and represented to the still believing though insufficiently instructed, people as an equally illegal and impious measure. And thus it suits the policy of these blind leaders, that the unfortunate people scarcely ever hear anything besides, except decidedly unchristian voices. If they hear, for example, that it is said that the spirit of the age must gain influence over the Council, they are the more inclined to follow blindly these blind leaders. For their Catholic conscience knows what is meant by the spirit of the age. What they do not know is, that a spirit of the age will indeed tyrannise over the Council, only it will be curialistic and Loyolistic, instead of being one of coarse materialism. They do not know that those upon whom suspicion is thrown, as being apostates or conceited fools, are exactly those Catholics who, in opposition to the wicked plot* which is being openly carried on, insist upon the great truth, that a truly Œcumenical Council ought to listen to no spirit of the age, but only to maintain faithfully what has been revealed by the Holy Ghost. *Observandum nobis magnopere est ante omnia, uti mandatum Dei et non nostras traditiones populo observandas tradamus*, &c.†

And how ridiculous is the constant reference to so-called Court theologians. As if there could be such persons. O merciful God! Theology in the present Courts and with the present Governments is a thankless profession. It brings neither honour, nor favour, nor even a morsel of bread. *On n'en a que faire.* Search for your Court theologians in the

---

* So it appears again from the impertinent work of the Roman Mgr. Nardi, who comes forward with all the deceitful assurance which is so peculiar to half knowledge.

† Concil. Lemovic, A.D. 1031.

Court of Rome, or rather among the curialists, for in Rome itself there is now-a-days a great want of even moderate learning, and what little there is belongs to the so-called Jesuits, while the other Orders, under the dominion of the Loyolistic spirit, are morally dead. The only Court from which weak theologians,—and such it is possible to be with great learning,—fear anything is the Court of Rome, to the mercy of which they are now abandoned without defence; it is also the only Court from which any thing can be hoped or expected by ambitious theologians, and from this sinful inclination no human knowledge or learning is a protection, however high and holy its object may be.

And how does that side, which now claims Catholicity for itself alone, expose its nakedness! For instance, in order to prove the pretended futility and falseness of the apprehensions entertained by the most faithful Catholics, who have a competent knowledge of their religion, they appeal openly and with a triumphant countenance to the fact that the

Bishops themselves, some few favourites of the Roman Court alone excepted, do not know what is to be deliberated upon. How is it possible then to be apprehensive? O blind ignorance or presumptuous hypocrisy! How are you compelled to bear witness against yourselves!

Where was it ever heard of in the Church that an Œcumenical Council had been arranged in this manner? When was such a bureaucratic rule heard of in the Church, which would be objectionable and pernicious for the government of a temporal state, even if the framers of it had in their way the best intentions? When was it thought possible for a Council of the whole Church to be convoked, without any one knowing why or wherefore? For general allocutions, like the Bull of Indiction of June 29, 1868, are no declaration of the object of such a Council. Where was a Council ever heard of, which is intended to be Œcumenical, and is only occasioned by a Loyolistic intrigue; which is an open secret, whose ultimate objects have been blurted out by a few Bishops who have already spoken openly on that side—either because their discretion is not as great as the favour they enjoy in Rome, or because it is thought good to prepare the public opinion of the uninitiated for the intended *coup*, in other ways than by the *enfants terribles* of the *Civiltà*, the *Laacher Stimmen*, the Ratisbon journals, Rudis' πέτρα *Romana*, and numberless productions of this contemptible but unfortunately, in our days, only too influential stamp? Who ever heard of a Council of which nothing is officially made known beforehand, except (1) the (now avowed) seventeen secret questions to the Bishops, which, apart from their bureaucratic and despotic tendency, are only remarkable besides for their want of importance; (2) the summoning of a certain number of arbitrarily selected scholars, of whom the few who are distinguished and are not at the same time thoroughgoing curialists have notoriously only been used as statisticians; (3) secret Committees, of whose operations the Bishops, and even the Cardinals,—except a few confidants of the *Curia*—know nothing more than may be known by every other human being who is in possession of his sound senses, and who knows how to use them, and does not disdain to do it for this purpose? This is surely enough to justify all apprehensions about the Council only too completely. For God will not be mocked, and if men go on sinning wickedly in reliance on His promises, He gives them over to what the Holy Scripture calls *reprobum sensum*, that is the reprobate mind belonging to the natural man.* How entirely different must the preparations for a truly Œcumenical Council have been! The subjects to be treated of must have been made known to all the world, communicated to the Christian Governments, and such as are living convictions in the mind of the universal Church. Instead of being got ready at Rome by secret committees and confidants of the *Curia*, they would have been thoroughly prepared by all the Bishops with their clergy in

---

* Rom. i. 28.

Diocesan Synods. We regret not having discussed and explained this more exactly in our little work.

We are however at all times ready for the fight, for the sake of the good cause, as long as it is of any use, provided only that a field is allowed us. For much may still be retrieved. However the intimations we have already given are at present sufficient for all who are willing and able to learn. Indeed the work of the great Bossuet, *Defensio Declarationis Conventus Cleri Gallicani*, is alone exhaustive and affords a real arsenal of weapons for the defence of this truth. We quoted from a defective edition in the first edition of our little work. We discovered this not long ago, while looking at this never refuted and irrefutable masterpiece in the Royal Library here, but there is no time to correct the quotation now in this second edition. But it matters not. The whole work must be read and studied. No one, who has not done this, can discuss or form an adequate judgment upon these important questions, and upon the authority of the

Councils of Constance and Basle, until the time when the latter forfeited its Œcumenical character. In relation to some matters, and particularly in relation to one, not then obsolete, Bossuet deals much too leniently with the curialistic system in this book; and in regard to the controversy of the pious Bishops, Pavillon and Stephen Caulet, against Louis XIV., he declares that, as reporter to the Assembly of the clergy of the Empire, he will not express an opinion in that place. That is the only point that can be found fault with in this immortal theological work. There are imperfections in the personal conduct of the author, the greatest of which, and the only one which had important consequences, proceeded from his too great respect for the Court of Rome, but they make no difference to the invincible strength of this work. The policy of the French Government at that time prevented the publication of this masterpiece, and it was only circulated in manuscript until the year 1743. It was first printed in that year, after the death of

Cardinal Fleury and the end of his unfortunate ministry, undoubtedly according to Bossuet's own manuscript, and in the last form which he gave it in the latter years of his important life, as has been proved by the Bishop and Cardinal de la Luzerne, in the present century, and likewise in an excellent contemporary French translation. In the places which we intended to cite, Bossuet points out among other things, in what consists the *unanimis consensus* and Tertullian's *consanguinitas doctrinæ* in respect of the doctrine of the Church, not of an opinion of the schools, of which it can always be shown when and how it became more or less predominant; furthermore, that the celebrated Letter of Pope St Leo, although received and subscribed by almost the whole of the Western and by the greater part of the Eastern Churches, was nevertheless again examined in the Œcumenical Council of Chalcedon, and only accepted after this examination, whereupon Leo himself, in his letter to Theodoret on the subject, acknowledges that his letter had been sanctioned and confirmed by the Council and had thus first become binding! He also shows how the decision of Pope Agatho, although received by the Sixth Council, was again examined independently by the Spanish Bishops, because that Church had not yet acknowledged the Council; and again, how the history of the second Council of Nice proves the curialistic system to be theologically untenable, and much more to the same purpose. But an analysis of this work of Bossuet's, which presents a firmly connected chain, is impossible in this place, and we can only repeat that the whole should be most earnestly studied by every Catholic, and also other works, abridged for those who are not theologians by the most excellent authors of France and Italy,—of which some have even the authoritative form of Pastoral Letters,—which are well known to us, but alas, scarcely to be procured in our days. Those which are still most easily obtained are, Bossuet's *Conference with Claude*, his *Exposition de la Foi Catholique*, and his *Avertissements aux Protestants*, which contain much bearing on this subject, and the work of which we have been speaking, either in the original Latin or in the French translation.

If we consider more closely the wishes and hopes about the Vatican Council, which have been more formally expressed by the best instructed Catholics of the present day, since the first publication of this little work, we are obliged to acknowledge with regret the absence in most cases of those deeper views about the last things, derived by Christian antiquity from the study of the Prophecies. In consequence of this defect, we find it too often forgotten, that it is by no means enough to suppress certain symptoms without combating the malady itself. Now, there are certain particular evils—such as the incapacity of the Church at the present time to maintain her true and inalienable rights against the State, while her sacred name is made use of to la claim to non-essential rights, which she has only possessed by accident and for a time—further the incapacity of the Church to maintain the truth with the invincible power which naturally belongs to it, against the general unbelief and demoralisation, in consequence of the faulty education of the clergy, which it is now desired to make more general and more irremediable—the estrangement of the life of believers from the true life of the Church, arising from estrangement between the clergy and the people—and, lastly, the Roman Index, which is as powerless against what is really pernicious as it is injurious to the Church, with all the mischief connected with it—all these particular evils are only symptoms of curialism. And curialism has run in our days into such a giddy excess, as to assert directly,— what was never thought of until the time of Gregory XVI.,—that the Infallibility of the Pope, speaking *ex cathedrâ*, is to be held as a dogma, and to wish to get this hitherto unheard-of assertion sanctioned by the Bishops for the benefit of the unlearned in religion,—a thing, never fully thought of until 1869. Only with the removal of this terrible, and in itself mortal disease, will the symptoms of it disappear, which they will then do of themselves; but no treatment of the symptoms will be of any use, while the disease remains.

At the time of the Holy Councils of Constance and Basle it was generally acknowledged, and invariably confessed in Rome, that a reform in the ministerial chief and in the members of the Church was urgently needed, that is, a return to the original purity and sanctity, without prejudice to the richer display of the form and acquisitions of a legitimate development.

This reform was prevented by the deceitfulness of the human heart.

In the following century there came in its stead a violent revolution, in whose terrible waves the Catholic Church lost half of her members, and very nearly lost many more.

As the age still possessed a deep foundation of strength and capacity of faith, religious bodies arose out of it. Even the community of the anti-Trinitarians of that time must still be reckoned as such, although they already denied the fundamental principle of Christianity.

There now awoke, in the portion of the Catholic Church that was saved, a lively zeal and wish for reformation. It was under conditions and auspices far more normal than is the case with the present Council, that the Council of Trent was assembled. But even in truly Œcumenical Councils, as in the whole life of the Church, human weaknesses show themselves, without prejudice to the Divine guidance, and these weaknesses often have perilous consequences. It had been so at Constance and at Basle; it was so again, although for the most part with an entirely opposite tendency, in the Council of Trent, which was begun and ended with so much labour. These consequences have culminated after nearly three hundred years of truly reformatory and truly Catholic efforts in the final stifling of this endeavour, and the victory of a contemporary and spurious effort, that is the Loyolistic, which has substituted a revolution for a reformation. Only it is a revolution which, like the one analogous to it in political life, has been carried through from above, a revolution of lawless absolutism; though there is this difference between them, that what, in political life which belongs merely to this world, under certain circumstances can be compared to a crisis in a bodily disease, in the divine life of the Church can only be a symptom of the deadliest malady.

This revolution is now to receive its sanction and crown in the eyes of the multitude, the conditions created by it are to be declared normal; and for this purpose a new dogma, which alters the whole orthodox Catholic teaching of the Church, is needed, that of the infallibility of her ministerial chief—not to speak here of other equally new dogmas, which are to slip in with it—and an entirely new code, completely superseding the ancient laws of the Church, which has been compounded in accordance with the pretended necessities of the times, and is now to be declared the only one in force for the future.

All this has been made known, and for all this public opinion is being worked upon, while Catholics are to be prepared for its reception and endurance. Officially, all is shrouded in the deepest obscurity, and no regard is paid to the most faithful children of the Church. And with these new forms of dogma and canon law they think to undertake the contest against the enemy without, and dream of conquering by these means an universal monarchy in the empire of mind, and, if not able quite to overcome the enemy, of dividing the sovereign authority with him for awhile.

As to what concerns the new dogmas, they are indeed alleged to be just conclusions from undoubted articles of faith. We will not lay the chief stress here on the point that even then they would still not themselves be articles of faith. We do, however, insist that they are not just conclusions from those undoubted articles of faith, which for 1830 years the Church has faithfully preserved, and has examined and secured on all sides in their deep mutual connection; nay, that they are intrinsically irreconcileable with the purity and safety of those undoubted articles of faith, and consequently must introduce a subversive element into the sanctuary of the treasure of true Divine doctrine entrusted to the Church.

But that this gigantic mystification will be attempted, is by this time clear to everybody. The means by which it is to be made possible prove it, and even the denials which are occasionally put forth only show the badness of the cause, as they can only deceive those who are quite incapable of understanding what is said and what is done. While "the pontifical secret" is appealed to with a truly cynical rudeness of expression, in order to insult our apprehensions, as a mere troubling oneself about unlaid eggs, this very proceeding, which is incompatible with the character of an Œcumenical Council, shows clearly enough what the Church has now to deal with. And while the

Roman party deny that they mean to attempt to set up the so-called infallibility of the Pope as a dogma, yet by writings like those of Nardi and the *Laacher Stimmen*, by deriding the Councils of Constance and Basle and arrogantly striking them out of the list of Œcumenical Councils, and by the announcement of additional and professedly more solid works upon the unfortunate theme of that pretended infallibility of the Pope, which are to have prelates and professors for their authors, they prepare the Catholic nations, who are now worse instructed than ever, for what is then intended to be imposed upon them as a *fait accompli* of the modern policy.

"*Imple facies eorum ignominiâ, et quærent nomen Tuum Domine.*"* Any one who has an upright heart and is acquainted with the matter, cannot doubt what is our opinion. Yet in conclusion we protest here once more expressly, that we remain steadfast in the acknowledgment of the very real primacy of St Peter and of the

* Ps. lxxxii. (Heb. lxxxiii.) 17.

Cathedra Petri, and of their sacred and salutary rights. These rights are so dear to us that we lament every attempted usurpation of them, and detest it as a depravation of what God has appointed. The real rights of the Primate belong to the *depositum fidei*, and can never be mistaken or denied or abandoned by a Catholic. But by the grace of God we will as little agree with those who carry the arts, the spirit, and the policy of an apostate world into the sanctuary of our God, and who, for their own pleasure and that of a world which is indifferent to all but its own ephemeral interests, shamefully forget the rights, the duties, the sorrows, the dangers, the wounds, the never to be enough lamented internal slavery of the Church, which is the flock of Jesus Christ, His dearly bought inheritance. And thus do we desire to serve the Father and our God according to that genuine and uncorrupted doctrine, which many presume to call a sect and an erroneous doctrine; and while it is rather they who err from the ancient doctrine, we hold fast to it faithfully and immovably. We submit ourselves to the free and genuine judgment of the Church: this only we acknowledge as binding, to this only we appeal.* May the day of her deliverance come quickly, the glorious day of the full manifestation of the Lord. Blessed is he that hath part therein.† For the present time, and while the court of the everlasting sanctuary is trodden under foot by the Gentiles, we must hope even against all hope,‡ and wait for the Lord, as the martyrs and confessors waited for Him, who are gone before us and who ever remain our examples.

* Acts xxiv. 14; xxv. 10, 11.   † Rev. v. 10; Tob. xiii.
‡ Rom. iv. 18; Job xiii. 15.

THE END.

www.ingramcontent.com/pod-product-compliance
Lightning Source LLC
Chambersburg PA
CBHW020302170426
43202CB00008B/468